HOW WELL

Chr

Which other current singing sensations worked along-side Christina on the "New Mickey Mouse Club"?

Who were some of her musical influences growing up?

In what country did Christina gain fame as part of the duct singing "All I Wanna Do"?

What does she like to do when she's not on tour?

What are Christina's goals for the future?

FIND OUT ALL THE ANSWERS—
AND MORE—
IN . . .

Christina Aguilera

Christina Aguilera

Anna Louise Golden

St. Martin's Paperbacks

CHRISTINA AGUILERA

Copyright © 2000 by Anna Louise Golden.
Cover photograph © Brian Rasic/Rex USA Ltd.

ISBN: 0-312-97534-1

Printed in the United States of America

St. Martin's Paperbacks edition / February 2000

10 9 8 7 6 5 4 3

Acknowledgments

Once again, and forever, I'm completely indebted to a wonderful agent, Madeleine Morel. We've worked together on a number of books now, and she's always there, on my side and relentless. With her there, I feel like the luckiest writer in America.

Jennifer Weis, my editor on this book, has given superb support, as has her assistant, Joanna Jacobs. I'm extremely grateful to them both for the work they've put into this. We might not have worked together before, but I hope this is the start of a long association.

A writer might work alone, but there's always a network of family and friends whose help is invaluable. My mum and dad are always brilliant, and it's lovely to receive the e-mails every day and know what's going on back home. Lee and Greg (happy 18th, Greg!), Kevin, Kevan, and a whole host of others who have indirectly contributed to this work. Last, but never least, a million kisses to L&G for always being a part of me.

The following pieces were very helpful in the creation of this book: "Teen Genie," by Janet Weeks, in *TV Guide*; "Genie Behind 'Bottle'" by Alisa Valdes Rodriguez, *Los Angeles Times*; "Christina Aguilera," by Larry Flick, *Billboard*; "From Mickey . . . to Genie," *YM*; "Uncorking the Genie," by Sophronia Scott Gregory and Hayes Ferguson, *People*, Sept 27, 1999; "The Magic Touch," by Marc Ehrman; "Christina's World," by David E. Thigpen, *Time*, August 16, 1999; "One Talented Teen," by Andy Smith, *Providence Journal*; MTV News interview; "Ex-Mouseketeer a Hit in Rat Race," by Arlene Vigoda, *USA Today*, February 1999; "Bottle Rocket," by Chris Willman, *Entertainment Weekly*, September 17, 1999; "Christina Aguilera," by Lori Majewski, *Teen People*, November 1999.

Introduction

The genie is out of the bottle, and there's no way she's ever going back in. Not now, when she's had a Number One single and an album that debuted at the top of the *Billboard* charts. There's no going back.

The genie, of course, is Christina Aguilera. The first thing you notice, of course, is hair, so blond, so cool . . . and then big blue eyes, so huge and sweet. She's nineteen and lovely, but more to the point, she has all the talent in the world in her voice. People have compared her to Mariah Carey, and it's a very fair comparison, even if Christina doesn't get as carried away in her high range. The girl can definitely sing.

From Staten Island to Pennsylvania to Disney, Japan, and Transylvania (yes, honestly), she made a name for herself all over the globe before coming home and making it so real on the charts. The song she sang in *Mulan*, "Reflection," was the kind of ballad she loves, and it helped her break through to the big time in America. Anyone who heard it couldn't fail to be moved by it.

It was certainly enough to make record companies perk up their ears, and chase after Christina's signature. And the result was the kind of thing dreams are made of.

"I'm so excited that my head is spinning!" she says now, and it's perfectly understandable. When you've had your first single spend five weeks at Number One, and your debut album enter right at the top of the charts, the world simply can't be quite the same place anymore.

Of course, all that is a major cause for rejoicing. But it's only the tip of the iceberg. The simple fact is that, with such a voice, Christina Aguilera is going to be around for a long, long time. This is the start of what will be a huge career. In a few years the people say "Christina who?" when you mention her name will have her records and know the words to her songs. She'll be a household name, the way Whitney and Mariah are now.

For now, though, what she's accomplished in 1998 is more than enough. It's quite the achievement for a "new" artist, although Christina has paid her dues to get where she is. She's been working toward this for ten whole years, since she was eight and first appeared on *Star Search*. But even before that there were school talent shows and home.

From there it was just up and up. At that time, Christina was living in Wexford, one of the suburbs of Pittsburgh, Pennsylvania, and becoming very well known around town by singing everywhere and anywhere she could. She sang the National Anthem at football games and hockey games. She knew she had talent, and so did her parents. They believed in her, and encouraged her to make the most of her gifts.

By the time she was twelve, she was more than ready for the next step. There was little else she could do around Wexford that she hadn't already done. She needed new challenges, something to push her harder. And she found it in Mickey Mouse.

The original *Mickey Mouse Club*, in the 1950s, was a television show familiar to millions. It had eventually gone off the air, but to a generation, the Mouseketeers were like family. It was a feeling Disney was keen to resurrect, and so *The New Mickey Mouse Club* was born. When it started, Christina was much too young to even think of auditioning. But by 1992 she had age and plenty of experience, and landed a part—which meant a move to Orlando, Florida, where the studio was based.

The New Mickey Mouse Club would prove to be an amazing incubator of young talent. Not only was Christina a part of the cast, there was also Britney Spears, who would reach her own fame and fortune the same year as Christina; Keri Russell, who found a television home playing the title role in *Felicity*; and Justin Timberlake and JC Chase, who'd both become massive stars all over the world as part of 'N Sync.

Christina was part of the gang at Disney for two years, which gave her ample opportunity to sharpen her singing and entertaining skills. But, great as it was to be working there, and wonderful as the rest of the cast was, eventually she needed to be able to push herself harder, and to concentrate on her singing.

That chance came not in America, but in Japan. The professionalism she'd learned in Orlando helped when she joined Japanese pop star Keizo Nakanishi to record a duet, "All I Wanna Do." Christina was also featured in the song's video, and toured with Nakanishi, performing to large crowds—hardly surprising, since the song was a major hit over there.

But 1995 didn't only see her becoming big in Japan. On the strength of the song, she was booked to appear at the Golden Stag Festival in Transylvania, Romania. She wasn't pursued by vampires, or even villagers with stakes, but she did manage to cause a riot.

One thing artists rarely do at a festival is go into the crowd. Yes, it's asking for trouble, but it also blurs the line between performer and audience. Christina, though, had no qualms about meeting her fans—while she was singing, which was pretty impressive, since she was only due to perform two songs. And by doing it, she upstaged people with a lot more experience than her, like Sheryl Crow and Diana Ross, who both had to follow her, and try and calm the crowd who'd become so excited when this girl joined them.

As a performer, it was something of a high point for Christina—at least so far. She was still basically an unknown, but she'd managed to get 10,000 people eating out of her hand—not bad when you're only fifteen.

From there, it was back to a relatively normal life, or as normal as life can get for someone with a remarkably mature voice and the ambition to do something with it. Her manager was trying to put together deals, but at that point the record industry wasn't interested in teenagers, not realizing the teen revolution that was about to break.

And then came the Backstreet Boys, who pushed open the floodgates, and made the people in suits realize that there was a massive audience out there for pop music, and that it was going to be bigger than "alternative" ever was. The Spice Girls followed up their international success by becoming huge in America, and demonstrating that Girl Power was a very real concept, not just a marketing slogan.

And it wasn't just in music that teens were coming to the fore. On television, too, shows about teens drew big audiences. *Buffy the Vampire Slayer*, *Dawson's Creek*, and plenty of others which didn't portray teens too simply, became both critical and audience favorites.

Christina was still back in Pennsylvania, waiting for her big break, living a normal life, but eager to really do something with her singing. That chance came when she was seventeen, at the beginning of 1998. Disney had a new cartoon in the works, *Mulan*, and was looking for singers to perform some of the songs. For one, "Reflection," they needed someone with a real range, who could reach a high E above middle C—not easy. Christina's manager knew the people at Disney, and arranged an invitation for her to audition for the soundtrack.

It was her passport to much bigger things—if she made the grade.

She needed to cut a demo, and do it quickly, while her name was still fresh in people's minds. There was no time to book a studio and arrange musicians, so, in her living room, Christina made her own demo tape. In the background there was a karaoke tape of Whitney Houston's "I Wanna Run to You," a song which would show Christina's range and control.

It was all done in one take. The first version was exactly what was needed. Her manager overnighted it to Disney. Within two days, she'd landed the gig of singing on the *Mulan* soundtrack—the perfect introduction for someone who was basically unknown in this country. She was whisked out to Los Angeles—to a *real* recording studio this time, to cut "Reflection."

That in itself would have been excitement enough, but it was as if Christina's time had arrived. Her manager had been talking to RCA Records for a while about his client. As soon as they learned she was doing a song for *Mulan*, the label offered Christina a deal. All of a sudden, the girl was really going places.

In reality, "Reflection" proved to be the perfect calling card for Christina. When the movie appeared in the middle of 1998, her song was singled out and released as a single, making the top twenty in the adult contemporary chart. And that meant Christina had to make some personal appearances on television, including

Donny & Marie and *CBS This Morning*—pretty exceptional exposure for a girl who'd yet to turn eighteen.

And then it was time to think about *her* album. To focus entirely on it, she left high school. Christina kept a very full schedule of classes at home and working on her music—both full-time jobs. But there was no doubt that the time was right, and it was just emphasized when fellow teen sensation Britney Spears went straight to the top of the charts. There was a hunger for good female singers with strong songs. Christina had the voice, and she was certain that the songs that were being picked were all great.

Of course, the summer of 1999 proved her to be quite correct. "Genie in a Bottle" crashed onto the *Billboard* chart and spent five weeks at Number One. Then, in August, *Christina Aguilera* debuted at the top of the album charts. Could life get any better?

In a way, yes it could. The previous twelve months may have been very odd for Christina, but it was also a perfect time inasmuch as she also managed to attend her high school prom and feel like a "real" person again. And then there were the movie offers, several of them, from people who just couldn't resist those eyes, that hair, and one of the longest, leanest midriffs ever made.

For now, though, she's turned them down. Her music is the happening thing, and that's what she's going to concentrate on. She could be for the new millennium what Mariah was to the '90s—the voice of her time, someone who can build and build, continuing to improve.

Teen voices and stars come and go—we all know that. There are the one-hit wonders, the fads that pass. But real quality sticks around. Talent gets a chance to mature and ripen. Christina has spent a long time paying her dues and learning her trade. When you see her on-stage now, that's the product of ten years' experience in show business, and it shows. She can handle an audience perfectly, be gracious and sweet. And from here she can only get better and better.

By establishing herself so quickly, she's going to be able to move ahead, to keep the audience she has now and expand upon it. Give her a couple more years, and Christina Aguilera really *will* be a household name, not just the girl in the video or with the great summer song. There's a long, long career ahead of her yet, and she knows it.

While she's very much a part of her generation, growing up on the same music as all the other teens, her music isn't all about the dance floor. Listen to her ballads and you hear what she can really do, how emotional her voice can become. The pop draws you in, but the slower songs keep you coming back, moved by her sing-ing—and that's quite a feat for anyone.

She's the newest star, but her light is going to stay bright for many years. She's been a fan of Mariah Ca-rey's for a long time, and maybe it won't be too long before the pair of them are singing duets. (After all, if Mariah and Whitney can sing together, why not?) That would be something of a dream come true for Christina, acceptance by the woman whose voice has helped in-spire her, the handing over of the crown from one gen-eration to the next. It's true, really, that apart from Mariah, no one handles ballads as well as Christina—and Mariah's sound has moved much closer to hip-hop over recent years.

While considering the details of Christina's life helps tell what she's done, it really doesn't tell you anything about who she is and what makes her tick. She has a lot of facets to her personality, and a lot of complexities. The kid from Staten Island who became the girl from Wexford, PA, and now the superstar has had an interesting life (and it will only get more interesting). And, like all of us, she's a mass of contradictions.

What sets her apart is that voice, that special instrument which has been God's gift to her (and she naturally thanks Him in her record). Other than that, in many ways she's an ordinary teen with ordinary interests—but one who's been focused steadily on her singing for a good ten years, starting off a lot earlier than most people know what they want to do with their lives. Which makes her lucky, in some ways. But it also means her life has been lived in something of a fishbowl as a performer—locally, nationally, and internationally.

To date, she has chosen not to fully express her Latina heritage, but she undoubtedly will one day. There's so much of her that remains to be explored, but there's so much she's already seen and done. (How many 18-year-olds have been smashes in Japan and Romania, after all?) And now, like the cherry on the sundae, it's all been topped by big hits and stardom at home.

It's been a short, busy road so far, and one well worth taking a look at. She's a very special person with a remarkable and rare talent. And it's going to be a very long time before it goes away—or she does.

Chapter One

Staten Island is almost the crossroads between New York and New Jersey. The ferry over from Manhattan is just a short trip, but it takes you past two symbols of America—Ellis Island, where at one time immigrants to the country landed, and the Statue of Liberty, whose flame offered hope of a new, better life to those about to enter the United States.

In many ways, Staten Island itself has more in common with New Jersey than with Manhattan. It's suburban, very different from the blare of the city across the water. There are houses, townhouses, apartment buildings, and strip malls (but only one real mall). The hipness of New York City could be a continent away for all it seems to touch life here. Many families have lived here for generations, and their kids will live here, too—it's almost like a small town, with all the history of any small place. Families know each other, and there's none of the sense of anonymity that you find in a huge city.

But there are also those who pass through, who will only make their home here for a short time. Some military families live here, since the housing is relatively cheap, and there's good access to both New York and New Jersey. That was certainly the case for Fausto Aguilera and his wife Shelly. He was stationed close by, and the Island offered reasonably priced off-base housing.

Born in Ecuador, Fausto was a member of the U.S. Army, which meant moving from place to place as his assignments changed. And Shelly was no newcomer to travel herself. She was born in Pennsylvania, in Wexford, a town that had gradually become one of the Pittsburgh suburbs as the city grew larger. From an early age she'd shown remarkable talent as a musician, both on violin and piano, and had been good enough to become a member of the Youth Symphony Orchestra, with whom she toured Europe.

The couple had met in large part because Shelly was studying to become a Spanish interpreter, and Fausto was able to help her, with Spanish being his native tongue. They fell in love, and married. Even though becoming an Army wife had meant plenty of changes for Shelly, she was happy with her life. Even more since she was expecting their first child, who was due close to Christmas, 1980. And that was another reason to find a place that truly seemed theirs—a home for their baby. So Staten Island seemed the ideal place, cosy enough for a new family, convenient to everything, with all the amenities close at hand.

Christina was born on December 18, 1980. Right from birth she had huge blue eyes, so clear and luminous that it was impossible not to notice them. Everywhere Shelly took her daughter, people would remark on them.

Almost as soon as she could talk, Christina could sing. By then she had a younger brother, Casey, born two years after her, and with a new baby in the house, she sometimes had to amuse herself. And that was easy—she'd sing, imitating all the vocalists she saw on television. It just seemed so natural to her, as if it was what she'd been born to do.

In the bath she'd use a shampoo bottle as a pretend

microphone. In her bedroom it was a hairbrush, or anything she could lay her hands on. Singing centered her.

It was probably just as well that *something* did, because in the life outside, there was constant movement. Since Fausto Aguilera was a soldier, he was subject to all manner of postings, and the family had to gather their things and move on time and again. The home in Staten Island didn't last long. It was followed by Florida, then Texas . . . but never long enough in any one place to put down serious roots.

"I've lived everywhere from Texas, to Japan for three years," Christina explains, "to New Jersey. I'm this traveling girl. My father was in the Army, so I guess I'm an Army brat."

Even if Christina didn't get the chance to make any really close friends, she still had her singing, and right from the start she showed a very precocious ability at it, which Shelly recognized (having been a musician herself) and encouraged. Christina wanted to sing for people. In fact, the girl would open her bedroom window and serenade strangers as they walked by on the street. If there was no one else around, "she'd surround herself with stuffed animals, and they'd be her audience," remembers Shelly.

Curiously, it wasn't so much the pop music that she heard on the radio that stuck with Christina, but the soundtracks of Broadway musicals, in particular *The Sound of Music*. By the time she was six years old, she knew the whole thing, every melody and lyric, and could sing it from start to finish—in fact, she often did.

Another thing that seemed perfectly natural to Christina was speaking in Spanish. Since it was her father's first language, and Shelly was fluent in it, Spanish was often spoken around the house. In fact, given her last name, many people assumed Christina was Latina—in fact, she's half Ecuadorian and half Irish American.

She never really sang in Spanish, though. In the 1980s, there was no Latin music on the charts. As soon as she was old enough, she was singing in public, everywhere she could, whether it was at block parties or amateur talent shows. Her gift had really developed, and she had a voice that sounded much older than her years.

When Christina was five, two more children joined the Aguilera household, twin girls named Rachel and Stephanie. Christina was really beginning to flourish. What she couldn't know at the time was that things were going to change so much in the next couple of years.

Some marriages are meant to last. Others seem doomed to failure. No one can say why it happens; there's no magic ingredient. Some couples stay together for the sake of their children. Others find it better to split up. But things weren't going well between Shelly and Fausto. There was tension about so many things. They could either start all over and try to make it work, or split up. When Christina was seven years old, Fausto and Shelly Aguilera decided to split up.

The problems Shelly faced were enormous. She had four kids, and no place to really call home, where she could raise them. She hadn't stayed in one place long enough for it to really feel right. About the only place she could think of that might fit the bill was her hometown of Wexford, which was now part of greater Pittsburgh. And that would mean moving in with her mother—but at the very least, it was a place to catch her breath, and figure out what to do next. More than anything, Shelly wanted a *real* home for her kids, someplace they wouldn't have to leave in a few months. She wanted them to enjoy the same kind of security and grounding she'd had when she was growing up.

Of course, it was strange to have them all cramped into Grandma's house, but there was a real family feeling about the place—everyone pitching in, with plenty of laughter and joy. And Christina still had the special area within herself where she could disappear: her music. More than ever before, Shelly used it to help bring her daughter out of herself. Christina was old enough to understand what had happened between her parents, and to be hit hard by it. Music would at least give her something to focus on, something bright and pleasant. She even pushed Christina a little to perform at all the local block parties, although, in truth, the girl didn't need to be encouraged too much. She was happy to be up there, singing for people and making them feel good, getting to use that voice of hers to full effect. She spent so many hours in her room singing perfectly content to do that, too—but watching an audience respond was a very special feeling.

"Kids used to come over and ask if I could play, and my mom would tell them that was my play, singing all by myself," Christina recalls. "I guess I was weird."

The little girl who could belt out Whitney Houston covers at suburban block parties soon got noticed, and it was just a matter of time before the local papers— always eager for human interest stories, especially when they feature children—began to write about her. In turn, that meant that a lot of people in Pittsburgh came to hear about Christina and her amazing voice—among them the mayor, who invited her to perform for him. Naturally, that brought even *more* coverage. Both the local NFL team, the Pittsburgh Steelers, and the local NHL team, the Pittsburgh Penguins, asked her to sing the national anthem before games. How could a girl with a yen to perform refuse offers like those? Even if she didn't fully realize it, this was the kind of thing that had always been at the back of her mind—entertaining people.

If there was a problem, it was that Pittsburgh wasn't exactly the capital of the entertainment industry. Singing for the mayor at sporting events—even major sporting events—was fine for now. But what about the future?

If anyone had the answer to that, it was Shelly. She'd been a performer herself, so she had some insight into the problem. And one of the first questions was, did Christina really need to do anything with her talent at all? She was still only eight years old; it wasn't as if she had to make great decisions about her future for a long time yet. Shelly wasn't about to push her daughter into anything. But if the girl wanted to see what she could do, that was a different matter altogether.

The two of them sat and talked about it, and what going for a singing career might mean—a lot of auditions, a lot of disappointment. And that wasn't even considering a lot of practice, and all the time taken away from being a normal kid.

It was the first time Christina had really had to think about what her gift might mean. Until now it was simply something she'd done so much that it was a part of her, a major facet of who she was. Of course, she'd seen herself as some kind of star, but not in real life—it was just a dream. Now, perhaps, she could do something to make her dreams into reality—if she wanted to work hard. Shelly emphasized just *how* hard.

The conversation made Christina realize just how driven she was by singing. It had become even more apparent since they'd moved to Wexford. Despite her parents' break-up, Christina still had her mom, her grandma, and her siblings. But the heart of who she was was her singing. And she understood that she really did want to do something with it, to be heard, to make people happy with her voice.

Her timing was good; just after she'd made her decision, the local paper announced that auditions were going to be held in Pittsburgh to appear on *Star Search*. The show is barely remembered today, but in the 1980s it was a major way for young talent to be heard. Hosted by Ed McMahon, who'd been Johnny Carson's sidekick on *The Tonight Show*, the syndicated television show drew a good-sized viewing audience. Some of the contestants had gone on to careers in show business. More than anything, for Christina, the idea of auditioning, then possibly appearing on and even winning the show, offered a way forward. She *had* to do it, and Shelly was behind her all the way.

Of course, there was a long way to go between starting regional auditions and actually appearing on the show. All over the country there were many thousands with the same dream, to a greater or lesser degree, and some of them, like Christina, had real talent.

A lot of kids entered the competition. Some were pushed along by stage parents, others had their own desires. And judges loved kids. They had that cute factor that was always a winner with audiences.

But Christina had a secret weapon that really set her apart from so many of the other kids who were auditioning around America: her voice. As soon as she opened her mouth to sing, it was hard to believe you were listening to someone who was only eight years old. Not only was there a real maturity in the sound, but also in her phrasing, and the pitch. She didn't waver—she hit each note dead-on.

Even then, Christina sounded as if every singer she'd ever heard had been absorbed into her skin. She could do ballads, blues, R&B, jazz—she felt it all. And when she was singing, she believed every word. It wasn't a song, it was her life for the few minutes she was singing, and that, too, would help make her unique. It was the kind of trait all the great singers possess: the ability to convince an audience that this is *their* story.

Christina believed in herself and her talent without every being cocky about it. Yet that didn't stop her from being nervous when she and Shelly went to the Pittsburgh audition for the show. The waiting room was crowded, and waiting around for such a long time to have her short time on stage only made her more nervous. This was unlike any appearance she'd done in the past, and she knew that a lot more was riding on it. She had to be good. Not just good, but the best.

Christina's turn eventually arrived, and with Shelly waiting in the wings, she marched out onto the stage. The spotlights were on her, hot and blinding. She knew there were people down there, waiting, but she couldn't see them—and maybe it was just as well. Her music began, and right on cue she began to sing, losing herself in the song the way she always did. It could have been her bedroom, not an important audition. Every time, she gave it all she could, and this was no exception.

When she finished, and bowed toward the darkness of the theater, there was just silence—but these guys were there to audition, not praise. If she made it past this round, that would be praise enough for Christina— at least for now.

The contestants had already been told that they'd be informed in the mail in a few days. Waiting was like torture, running home from school each day to check the mail and see if there was any word yet. Finally the envelope arrived, and mother and daughter tore it open to learn that Christina was one of the few to pass on to the next round. She'd succeeded!

Success was all relative. She'd made it past the first round. What that meant was that she'd be up against other winners, so the competition was going to be a lot stiffer. But there was that light at the end of the tunnel, the chance to appear on national television, and show just how good she was.

At school, some of her classmates were thrilled for her, while others just seemed jealous, as if she was maybe getting big-headed by winning. But Christina never made it seem as if she were better than anyone else. She simply had this gift, and it was her duty to make the most of it. If that meant pushing herself hard, then that was the way it had to be.

For the next round, she and Shelly would have to travel, and stay overnight. It wasn't Los Angeles, where the show itself would be taped, but it was still something of an adventure. Since settling in Wexford, Shelly hadn't wanted to take her kids on any road trips. Apart from the expense, there was just the feeling of being settled in one place. But Christina had got a feel for traveling early on, and she loved going to a different city and checking into a motel; it made her feel like a star.

Even that feeling, though, didn't make waiting around to perform any easier. This time the other singers were of a much higher quality, and though Christina knew she had an extraordinary talent, the fact was that she was still only eight, and was going to have to pull out something very special to impress against the older girls.

Could she do it? Did she have it in her, at such a

young age? Christina knew she couldn't afford to have any doubts. She was as good as all the others—no, better—and she was just going to blow them all away with her singing. She got on the stage and once again vanished into her own world of songs, only coming back to earth as the last notes finished behind her. She really had no idea how well she'd done, or what had happened in the last few minutes; she'd gone off to another place, completely lost herself in what she was doing.

This time all the contestants were told on the spot whether they'd made it through or not, which meant less waiting; still, the nerves just jangled for what seemed like forever until the judges announced their results. There were a lot of tears, and plenty of glum silence. And for a few, there was the joy of triumph.

When Christina's name was spoken as one of the winners, it was by far the biggest moment she'd experienced in her life so far. She'd gone up against really good singers, older singers, and won her way through. And it meant she was going to head to the West Coast for the first time in her life, to see L.A. and be on national television. It was all pretty amazing, but very, very cool.

The airline tickets and the hotel were paid for by the show, or at least its sponsors. To Christina, it was real luxury to have a driver waiting for her and her mother at LAX, ready to take them to the hotel. This was the way stars lived all the time. This was the kind of thing that could happen if you won *Star Search* and went on from there to the real big time. She liked it.

They had their first night free, to relax a little and do some sight-seeing. There was dinner, then out to see the Hollywood sign and all the landmarks that made the city so special. It was a wonderful time for both Christina and her mother. Sleep was hard to come by, but eventually it arrived.

The next day was the big one. A rehearsal in the morning, and then taping the show in front of a live audience later in the day. Everyone got to meet Ed McMahon, and there were long run-throughs for all the contestants. It was exciting, true, but at the same time it was boring— endless repetitions, and all kinds of technical problems to be overcome. However, it did give Christina a chance to size up the other singers. They were good. Very good. But she knew she was too, and that she was in with as much of a chance as any of them.

She'd been nervous before, but it was nothing compared to the way she felt at the taping. This was it, the cameras trained on her, people in the theater watching her, and the knowledge that in a few weeks millions of people around the country would be watching her and making their own assessment of her talent. And there was the panel of judges, the people she had to win over.

After taking forever earlier, now it all seemed to go by in a blur. She knew she'd been onstage, but suddenly she was back with her mom, waiting with everyone else for the results. Finally they came through. Christina was second in the singing. A girl four years older than her had won. At first, it didn't seem fair—the other girl *was* older, after all, and she began to cry as Shelly hugged her. To have come this far and then to lose . . . it just didn't seem right. These days she can laugh and say, "I think I'm over it," but at the time it was totally devastating, as if her entire world had fallen apart. And in a way, it had. She'd been so focused on this, so certain that this was meant to be, that losing hadn't occurred to her. And now her mom picked up the pieces as they spent a quiet, gloomy night before flying back to Pennsylvania the next day.

Some of the kids at school were sympathetic. After all, she was from Wexford and she'd made it onto television singing, which was awesome. Others resented her having any kind of success at all.

Christina was astonished that some of her classmates—along with older kids and their parents, resented her singing and making it to *Star Search*. What was the problem? Some of the kids in school began ignoring her, as if she'd become some kind of outcast, and that just made her sad. She still had her friends, but why was all this happening?

And that was hardly the worst of it, although it was bad enough. She could take people being mean. She and her family could laugh that off as stupidity and jealousy, because other kids couldn't sing as well as she could, and resented the fact that she had talent. She could understand that. But when the tires of her mom's car were slashed, that was something else altogether. That went way beyond just jealousy. Of course, they called the police, but there was little they could do. No one was about to fess up to the vandalism, and there weren't any clues—it could have been almost anybody.

Before, Christina had been glad to talk about her singing. She was happy to show off the newspaper clippings about herself. She was proud of them, and she believed she had a right to be. Now, she turned inward a bit. It was harder to trust other people, because you never knew when they'd turn around and ignore you, or do something really dumb and hurtful. She was safe with her mom, her grandma, her brother and sisters. They would never let her down.

So, while there was plenty of love at home, it was

hard for Christina not to feel more and more isolated. She felt hurt and betrayed, but it did make her value her family and the people who'd stuck up for her even more than she had before. Now she knew who was on her side. And all of this—losing on *Star Search* and everything that had happened after she got home, made her really determined to have a career as a singer, if only to show them she could. She had the ability, of that much she was sure, and now she'd acquired the drive to make it all happen. Even if it took her years and years, she'd show them all, and make her family really proud of her. She'd already learned that it wouldn't be easy, but that was okay; she was more than willing to work hard at it. And it would happen.

She was so determined to make it happen that she took the money she'd won as a runner-up on *Star Search* and used it to buy a small portable public address system so she could entertain people on the block, in the park, wherever she could haul it. It was an unusual thing for a girl to do, but it was what Christina wanted. It showed how committed she was to singing, and how she wasn't going to let anything stop her from achieving what she saw as her goal in life.

Chapter Two

It was 1989. Christina was eight, and knew what she wanted to do with her life. Life in Wexford hadn't been easy for her since *Star Search*. It was almost as if she'd done something wrong by trying to put the place on the map. She had dreams, and she was trying to follow them. It wasn't her fault that the other kids didn't have their own dreams yet.

The problem was that the world wasn't crying out to hire young singers who hadn't won on *Star Search*. It sounded great that she'd made it there, but within the business it really didn't count for anything. There were still the block parties, and chances to sing the national anthem at sporting events, but that wasn't what she wanted to do with her life. Christina had had a taste of something bigger, and she wanted more of it.

But how? She lived in Pennsylvania, not Manhattan, or Los Angeles, or even Orlando, where the Disney Channel was based. There was simply nothing going on here. All she could do was practice as much as she could, and hope to take advantage of those few opportunities that did come her way.

At least she was getting some semblance of a normal childhood. If she'd lived in one of those major cities, there'd have been a constant round of auditions—her life would have revolved around trying out for different shows. This was much healthier, as Shelly fully understood. And Shelly had other responsibilities. There were three other kids who needed her. Christina couldn't have *all* the attention, even with her very special gift.

And Christina wasn't totally without friends. There were girls she could play with, places she could go. She had fun, although when it came to singing she was deadly serious. She listened to the radio a lot, and her mom's record collection, taking it all in, so that at some point she could use it in her voice. Sometimes it was hard to think of her as a child, particularly when Shelly heard her practicing, working so hard to become perfect. In music, it seemed, she was even more driven than her mom had been.

Singing had truly become Christina's passion, her retreat from the world. When she was lost in a song, nothing else could touch her. She could forget how some of the kids ignored her, the way they looked at her. Everything vanished, and only the tune and the words existed. There was a magic about it—it cast a spell over here, made her feel remarkable, and so good that she knew doing this was right.

Of course, when she finished, and came back to earth, all the old problems and heartaches were waiting for her. But she felt stronger, more able to face them. And one day singing would take her away from them all, and they'd never bother her again.

Still, she was eager to do more, and move ahead a little. Losing on *Star Search* had been a massive disappointment, but she was getting over it. Not only did she have Whitney Houston to look up to as a singing role model, but Mariah Carey's first album had been released, and that was nothing less than a total revelation.

"I have a love for Mariah Carey," Christina says now. "Her style and technique is amazing."

It gave her something more to aspire to. She might have been known around Pittsburgh as the little girl with the big voice, but she wanted to be known that way all over America. But how?

The possibility came when she was nine. Disney was looking for performers for a show provisionally titled *The New Mickey Mouse Club*. And singers were really needed. Open auditions were going to be held all over the country—including one in Pittsburgh. It was the sort of show for which Christina would be ideal. And the fact that they were holding auditions so close to home almost made it seem like fate. There was absolutely no way she would miss this.

Her mother warned her not to get too excited—that there would be thousands and thousands of kids from all over the United States trying out for the show, but Christina hardly listened. She just knew in her heart that this was going to be her big break, that it was meant to be.

There were a total of ten spots open on the show for kids, and the producers would end up seeing some twenty thousand kids around the country. In other words, the odds against any one performer actually getting to the show were pretty massive. But for those who made it, the reward would be huge. They'd be on television every week, with what amounted to a guaranteed audience of kids their own age and younger who watched the Disney Channel. And who knows where it might go from there? The sky was the limit. You only had to look, for example, at Annette Funicello, one of the stars of the original *Mickey Mouse Club*. She'd forged a career making records and in the movies. It could happen to them too, if things went well.

All over the country, kids and their parents were preparing for three minutes in the spotlight, a chance to strut their stuff. By the law of averages, many would be mediocre at best. That would help the good ones shine even more. But paring down those good ones to just ten . . . now that was going to be a rough job. And even the best ones might not make it, depending on their screen tests. You could be the best singer on the world, but if you didn't come across on television, you didn't have much of a chance. You had to be a *performer*, too.

There were a number of categories, including dancing, but it was the singing that interested Christina; that was where her talent lay, and with the audition coming up rapidly, she worked extra hard on her material and her presentation.

It felt different from *Star Search*. In a way, she was less nervous—after all, she'd been on television now, and faced the camera. But in a way she was more nervous, because this seemed much bigger to her, and somehow more important, possibly because it was the first opportunity that had come to her since her loss, and it was vital she really make something of it. She needed it to make herself feel as if she were doing the right thing, committing so much of herself to music.

The day of the audition, she was calm on the outside—after all, she was experienced, she'd done this kind of thing before—but seething on the inside. She knew she was still very young compared to many others, but there were also plenty of kids her own age. She and Shelly seemed to spend an eternity waiting for her time on the stage, when she'd get up there, give her music to the pianist, and compose herself under the spotlight. She was going to sing what had become her special number, the one they loved at the block parties—Whitney Houston's "I Wanna Dance with Somebody." It showed her range, and also the way her technique was remarkably advanced for her age.

She belted the song out, loud and brash, making it seem a little bluesy—she'd listened to her mom's old Etta James records, and loved them—something a little different from the way most girls would be singing. She was one of over five hundred trying their luck that day in Pittsburgh, and she knew it wouldn't be easy. But she gave it all she had, and trusted in her own ability to make it all happen.

When the song was over, and the last chords had died away, she left the stage feeling happy. She'd done her very best, and she knew she'd done well—very well, in fact. From here on in, it was out of her hands, but there was no reason to think it wouldn't go well. On the drive home she'd talk for a while, then fall silent, then talk again. Once again, all she could do now was wait.

Waiting was always the hardest part. When you're young, a day can seem so long that a week, two weeks, a month seem to drag on and on and on. Every day she checked the mail, but there was nothing, not even a form rejection letter.

Then, finally, it came. But it wasn't the amazing news she'd hoped for. Christina hadn't made the final cut for one of the spots on the show, or even for screen testing. But she'd done well, and would be considered if a place came up later.

She was devastated. She really thought this would be it, that she was meant to be on *The New Mickey Mouse Club*. But she'd been wrong. Obviously, her instincts had been wrong. Maybe they'd been wrong about her singing, too, and she just wasn't cut out for all this. Maybe she should just try to be a normal kid, so everyone wouldn't hate her for having ambition.

It was a depressing time. School wasn't much fun, and at home she felt as if she'd let herself and her family down a little. She'd had such high hopes, and they'd been dashed. The opportunity for something like this came so rarely that to have missed out made her feel as if she'd failed, although her family and friends did everything they could to make sure she didn't feel that way.

She really didn't believe she'd ever hear from Disney again—she assumed it was just something they wrote to everyone who'd tried out. So what should she do now? She seriously considered quitting singing, but after talking with her mom, she knew that she couldn't do that. It would be like cutting off a part of herself. She'd been singing for so long, and it made her feel so good, that stopping would just be dumb. And it wasn't as if she had to sing for other people to make herself happy. It was good just in her room, looking in the mirror and holding a hairbrush. Not the same, perhaps, but still a relief and a release. And in the end, that was the most important thing.

So things went on as they had before. There was school, and summer. Hanging out with friends, going places with her brother and sisters, being around her mom and grandma. And there was more to the family, too. Shelly had been dating a man she'd met, a paramedic in Wexford called James Kearns, whom everyone called Jim. After her divorce it had taken a few years before she was ready for another relationship—particularly as she had the kids to raise—but she knew now that this was the real thing. Jim knew and loved the kids, and they loved him as well. Finally Shelly announced that she and Jim were going to marry, and everyone was very happy for her. He would become a real father for the family and would prove to be as big a supporter of Christina's talent as Shelly. With the joy of her mom's new marriage, slowly the pain of not making it with Disney faded a little, although she felt it every time she tuned in to *The New Mickey Mouse Club* or saw an ad for the program. It could have been her. . . .

What she had to do was consign all that to the past, move on, and be happy. For the most part, she was. Who knew what might come up in the future? And she wasn't exactly *old*. As Shelly pointed out, there'd be lots of chances in the future, and she'd already had the kind of experiences most kids her age couldn't even imagine. So she daydreamed about the day she'd become a star, when the photographers would be snapping her picture, when she'd feel glamorous, driving up in a limo, when her records would be out and she'd be hearing herself on the radio. It was a dream, but it seemed so real, as if it were just waiting to happen. . . . But who could tell the future?

She settled comfortably into a routine, singing for pleasure, playing, studying—and that looked as if it would be that for quite a while. And it was, at least for two more years. She'd grown a bit, and her voice had grown with her. It was 1993, and she was twelve years old, but she sounded more like twenty.

It's true to say that you never know what life has in store for you. There's something unusual waiting for every one of us around the next bend, and Christina was no exception. She had plenty of hopes for the future, but she had shelved them for a while. It made her more acceptable in Wexford to be like the other kids, not always talking about her grand singing dreams. She just kept those to herself.

One thing she'd certainly given up on was Disney. She didn't believe she'd ever hear from them again. In her mind, the ones who'd made it were lucky, and she'd have loved to have been one of them. But it hadn't worked out, so there was no point in worrying about it anymore.

So when there was a letter waiting one day, with a Disney logo on the envelope, she was more than astonished. While her mother waited, Christina opened it up and read it. And then she read it again, and a third time, before it sank in and she began screaming. They wanted her to screen test and possibly join *The New Mickey Mouse Club.* Two years after her audition, she was going to get her chance! It really was like something out of a fairy tale.

At least she'd kept up her singing, that was something. In fact, she sounded much better than she had two years before—more mature, and even more in control of the song.

There were plenty of details to be figured out—when could they get down to Orlando for her screen test? What should she wear? Should she get her hair cut? What should she sing? But details were what they were. The important thing was that Disney hadn't forgotten about her after all. They'd kept their promise, and someone in Florida had remembered the remarkably talented girl in Pennsylvania.

There were two weeks to go before her screen test, and Christina wondered if she'd have everything ready in time. She hadn't told the people at school, even though she simply wanted to bust with excitement. After what had happened before, she knew it was simpler just to keep everything to herself. If she made it—when she made it, she corrected herself—she could tell them then. And if, by some chance, she failed the screen test, well, they didn't need to know about that.

She was singing every spare minute now. She and Shelly had been to the mall to buy her some new clothes. There was an appointment with the hairdresser set for right before they left. The last time around, she'd felt so certain it would all happen—now she had to believe it was fate that had just taken a long time to catch up with her.

On the plane down to Orlando, Christina felt nervous, but they were nerves of anticipation, not fear. Somehow all this just felt right, so perfect. And she'd been in front of the cameras before; those didn't worry her one bit. At the airport, a car was waiting to take them to the hotel. There were passes to all the attractions, including Disney World, and they spent the next day there, treated like VIPs, going on the rides and forgetting that there was an audition the following day. There were shows and entertainers all over Disney World, and Christina had to admit the standard was high. If these people were performing in the theme park, and maybe not good enough for the TV show, what was the television quality like? Still, she knew in her heart she was going to do it.

Even so, she didn't sleep well that night. Her mind was racing. This was important, very important. It made her realize how unimportant her experience on *Star Search* had been. Finally she drifted off, only to have morning come much too early. She showered, but wasn't too hungry for breakfast; there were butterflies fluttering through her stomach.

The car picked them up and took them to the studio.

The complex was huge, and Christina wondered how people ever managed to find their destinations. Finally they reached the soundstage where *The New Mickey Mouse Club* was taped. The set was up, and other sets were scattered around the studio. Christina met the people who would be auditioning her. This time there was no line of people to be seen, only her. She was treated like royalty.

The lights and cameras were set and the director was in the control booth. There was no piano accompaniment this time, but a full tape backing for her song. She was given her mark, and from there it was up to her, to hope that the camera would love her.

Finally everything was ready, and the order was given for quiet on the set. Then it was action, the music started, and she was ready for it, smiling, happy, in her element. Her three minutes seemed to pass both in a flash and to last forever. She felt as if she were outside herself, watching Christina perform, even as she was lost in her song.

Then it was over, and she felt drained, having given it her all. Shelly came over and hugged her, and they sat down and waited. This time it wouldn't be a letter in the mail, or even a phone call, but they'd know here and now, once the tape had been played back.

The few minutes dragged on and on. Christina began to wonder if they'd forgotten about her and moved on to something else. But eventually the door to the room opened and the director and producer walked in. They were smiling.

They asked if she wanted to join the cast. Without even missing a beat, she was screaming "Yes!" And that was all she needed to know.

Well, maybe not *all*, but for now those were the only

words in her head. The executives and Shelly sat down and started discussing things. There were contracts to be signed. It meant that, for the first time in her life, Christina was going to be paid for her singing, although she'd happily have done it for free. She was twelve, and she could call herself a professional singer. Now *that* was so cool.

When they flew home the following day, Christina could barely contain herself. The excitement was bubbling out of her. They'd called home the night before and told the rest of the family the good news—but they'd cautioned everyone not to go spreading the word. Once bitten, they were now twice shy about letting people know Christina was a success.

On the plane home, Shelly explained to her daughter how everything would work with the show. She'd been worried they might have to move down to Florida, which would have uprooted the family just after they all finally felt settled and secure. But it wouldn't have to be that way. While some of the cast members did live in the Orlando area with their families, more flew down for rehearsals and taping. Since a whole season of shows was filmed during the summer, Christina wouldn't even have to miss any school. Shelly and Christina would spend her summer break down there. It would mean a lot of work, but then she could go home, and go back to school as if nothing had happened. She wouldn't need to be a full-time showbiz kid with tutors and all the rest. She could live a normal life. Or as normal as her life could be from now on.

It was like having the very best of both worlds. She could still be Christina, and spend time with the friends she'd made in the town she'd become used to, and she could also be a singing Mouseketeer. It was a good deal.

The money she made appearing on the show would be put aside for college. It was just like having a really big summer job, really. Except people wouldn't see her work until she was finished with it.

The New Mickey Mouse Club had been on for a few seasons, and had acquired a good solid audience of kids who tuned in week after week. In part, they were there because it was a Disney show with great production and strong family values. But it was also because the cast had become something like friends. They were familiar. That meant Christina was going to be the new kid on the block. There was a lot she had to learn and assimilate before summer rolled around and she headed back to Florida. But that was fine. Now she had a goal.

Among the group of Mouseketeers were Britney Spears, who was a year younger than Christina, Joshua Scott Chasez, who was called JC or Josh by everyone, Justin Timberlake, who was also a year younger than Christina, and Keri Russell. All of them would go on to major fame in the years to come. But for now they were part of the clique that made up the Club. And every time Christina turned on the television to watch them, she knew that in a few months it would be her face up there too.

There were still weeks of school to go through before summer vacation, though. Keeping her secret to herself was almost impossible for Christina. She wanted to tell *everyone* what had happened to her. Inside, though, she knew that wasn't a smart move. It was more prudent to keep quiet, and let them find out later. So she kept her own counsel, worked hard, and spent every spare minute rehearsing, doing vocal exercises—everything she could do so she'd be ready to make the best possible impression in Florida.

For right now, as her mother told her, Christina's job
was to keep good grades. School always had to come
first, no matter how important the show seemed. So
Christina did the best she could. The last day of the
school year was circled on her calendar, though, and she
was just counting down the days until it was over and
her real life could begin.

Finally, she was going to have a chance to show
everybody. The ones who made fun of her back when
she'd lost on *Star Search* wouldn't be able to do that
now. But she wasn't going to try to lord it over them.
She wouldn't say a word; she wouldn't need to. They'd
be able to see her every week on their television screens.
When someone asked what she was doing for the summer, she just said she was going to Florida, and left it
at that.

It was always possible that the Disney gig could lead
to bigger things, but she wasn't even thinking about
that—*The New Mickey Mouse Club* was about as big as
she could imagine for herself, and it seemed pretty major, something huge in her imagination. To be one of
the chosen few . . . well, it was amazing. Above everything else, it meant that people who really knew about
these things thought she could sing, a vindication of all
the work, the practicing, all the block parties and the
disappointments she'd gone through. She really did have
talent.

May was humid, and it was hot early in June. At
school everybody had that end-of-the-year feeling, ready
to be free for a while. Christina had it even more than
most. Her mother wouldn't let her pack yet, but she already knew exactly what was going into her suitcase,
and she was going to be ready to get out of town just

minutes after the final bell had rung. The future was calling, and she was listening, and waiting with open arms. It seemed as if she'd been waiting forever for this to happen, and now it was *so* close.

Chapter Three

Finally it was summer. But to Christina it wouldn't really be summer, it wouldn't all be happening, until she got off that plane in Orlando. She'd been born to do this. Unlike JC Chasez, who claims that "I didn't start singing until I got to Orlando with *The Mickey Mouse Club*" (he'd really started out as a dancer), Christina was primarily a singer. But she'd be doing more than just that on the show. As JC points out about his own Disney experience, "It was one of the best things I could have done. I got to get my fingers into everything—I wasn't restricted to one thing at all. I got to do comedy, which was fun, and I got to do all kinds of music. If I could do it again, I would."

What none of the cast knew at the time was that the show was entering its last two seasons, so Christina would be one of the final additions to the cast, getting in the door just in time.

Naturally, she wondered how the other members of the cast would accept her, but that quickly proved to be no problem. Although they already knew each other well, they were quick to welcome the new, rather nervous girl on the first day, and make her feel at home. In particular, Christina struck up an immediate friendship with Britney Spears, who was a year younger than her, but somehow seemed older, because of her experience on the show. Contrary to a lot of rumors flying around,

Christina and Britney remain very good friends. At the party following a recent awards show, Britney insisted on hanging around the stairs until she saw Christina arrive, so they could have plenty of time together.

Back then, though, Christina was feeling her way. She and Shelly had moved into a fairly sparse apartment for the time they'd be in Florida, leaving the other kids in their grandma's care back in Pennsylvania—they'd come down later for a vacation. By the end of the first day, she felt as if this were where she belonged. It had been all rehearsals, and very exhausting, but thrilling too. She'd had a chance to sing, and everyone had been impressed by her voice, just as she'd been impressed by their talents. And she also had a chance to try herself at other things, a little bit of dancing, a little bit of comedy, and discovered she liked those, too. The kids she worked with were all professionals, but very cool. There was no attitude. And that was the way it would remain for the two seasons she was with the show.

"There was some crazy things that happened on the set," she remembers fondly. "People were always telling jokes, playing pranks and stuff like that, but . . . I have to keep certain things secret." For all their professionalism, they were still a bunch of kids, and they weren't afraid to be kids when they weren't working. On the set, though, work was what it was all about, and every one of them gave their all. They all really wanted to be there, and to do the best they could, showing what they could do and helping each other.

Arriving home that first night, Christina was exhausted, more tired than she'd been in her entire life, it seemed. But she felt great. She couldn't stop smiling. This was what it was all about. And five days a week, that was how it would be for the entire summer. The kids would work and work (for as long as the laws allowed, no longer) to prepare a show and then tape it. The weekends, at least, would be free. When Christina wasn't hanging out with her mom, she'd be off with other members of the cast. Some of them lived in Orlando, and knew all the cool places to go in the city. In a way it was like visiting friends.

More than that, it was a summer in which Christina learned a lot. She thought she could sing well, and believed in her talent, but there were others on the show— like Britney—who sang as well as she did. There was also the chance to work with vocal coaches, who helped her with her technique, her breathing, things that could only help her improve. And even to her own ears, there was a rapid improvement in her phrasing.

Being somewhere else also exposed her to lots of different kinds of music. There were the other kids she worked with, but there was also the radio, and just the general vibe around. All the sun and heat seemed to make people looser and happier. There was a lot of Latin music in the air, and that was pretty cool. She'd never really been exposed to it before, but she really liked it. And, as her mom pointed out to her, it was part of her heritage on her father's side, even if she didn't look the slightest bit Latin.

She also began to hear older soul and funk from the '60s and '70s, artists like Aretha Franklin and Chaka Khan, who'd influenced people like Whitney and Mariah. But that was the way you learned. You started off admiring people, then slowly moved on to the work of the people who'd influenced them. And through her mother she discovered older R&B, and it all clicked together. It would help Christina become a more soulful singer as she listened and learned more, absorbing things through her skin, it seemed, and bringing them out in her own way, in her own voice, sounding, in the end, like no one but her.

It was quickly becoming a magical summer for her. Tiring as it was, every aspect of the work was thrilling. This wasn't a job, it was a real adventure, and she found herself becoming an entertainer, not just a singer, which was something she'd never expected or even thought about.

For her, music was becoming a journey, on which she was constantly discovering new and exciting things. It felt as though she'd come alive, between really getting into music and appearing on *The New Mickey Mouse Club*.

She felt as if she'd suddenly grown from being a kid to a young woman, finding out more about herself and the world. Yes, it was a summer away from home, with quite a lot of freedom—even if she was spending a lot of her time working—but there was more to it than that. She could feel herself growing inside.

Dancing and acting didn't come as naturally to her as singing, but there were people to help her. Not only coaches, but other members of the cast, whose main abilities lay in those areas—people like JC or Keri Russell, who were always willing to take the time to work with others. And that was one of the things that made the Disney experience so enjoyable—everyone was so cool. They had time for jokes or to offer advice. Christina was automatically accepted as one of the club, one of them, just by virtue of the fact that she was there.

By the time the rest of the family came down, Christina almost felt like a native. Her friends had guided her around town, and she'd been to Disney World so many times she almost knew the place with her eyes closed (getting in there was one of the best perks of working for Disney), so she was able to show her brother and sisters around.

There was still work to do, more shows to be taped before the summer was over and school began again. Even though it was so strenuous, she realized that it didn't seem like work at all. She was having fun, she'd made a whole new set of friends—and she was getting to sing a lot. Life really didn't get any better than this, she decided. How could it?

Of course, it would all end soon enough, but she didn't want to think about that until she absolutely had to. This was the best thing that had happened to her in her entire life. Maybe it was the fact that they were all focused on the same thing, that they all had remarkable talents, but she'd made a special bond with the other members of the cast. There was another pretty new kid, too, Justin Timberlake, and Christina befriended him. Like her, he'd been a contestant on *Star Search,* although he hadn't made it past the first round of auditions. Just a month younger than Christina, they soon became great buds. No one was going out as boyfriend or girlfriend; they all just worked together and hung out together. It was like having twelve best friends, of both sexes.

Eventually, though, the summer did have to end, and it was time to pack up and prepare to return to Wexford. It was home, and her family was there, but there was a part of Christina that just wanted to stay in Orlando, where people accepted her for who she was and what she could do. Saying goodbye to everyone was very difficult. They'd all become so close by working together. In particular, Christina and Britney had become really good friends, the kind to keep in close touch, although she knew she'd call the others and write them too. They'd shared something special. Not unlike going to camp, but more intense.

Packing up her stuff, she found there were all kinds of souvenirs and photographs that would help keep the experience alive and fresh in her mind until next summer rolled around and she was back in Florida again. That was something to look forward to, even if it seemed a long way away right now.

She dreaded going back to school, and having to face her classmates. There were her friends, of course, but she knew what was going to happen as soon as word got around that she was on *The New Mickey Mouse Club*. A lot of kids would become jealous and ignore her, others would hate her. It just wasn't right. Her friends—her real friends—could be happy for her. Why couldn't everyone else?

At least there'd be a few days—the long Labor Day weekend—before she had to go back to that. She could relax with her family and get used to her own bed again. In some ways it really would be good to be home, surrounded by her own stuff after pretty much living out of a suitcase for a couple of months. But after the time she'd spent really singing, going back to just doing it in her bedroom, with a hairbrush instead of a real microphone, was going to seem weird, and unreal. She'd been there, she'd done it properly. Going back to performing for a mirror just didn't feel right, somehow.

At least she could carry on learning about music, and in particular about different singers. There wasn't much chance to go and see shows, particularly since she was only twelve, but that was okay. She bought CDs and listened. Music was still the main thing in her life. And she was beginning to be very glad it was there.

Finally it was time to take a cab to the airport, and look out the window at Orlando for the last time, to wave goodbye to what had been a pretty major and way cool summer. She'd be back again next year, she knew. It wasn't really the end of the world. So why did she feel like it was?

Dreading the return to school was one thing. Actually going was another. Yes, she felt deflated to be back in junior high after such a wonderful summer. But by not telling anyone what she'd done over the last couple of months, at least things were the way they had been for a while—which was tolerable. The news would get out sooner or later, she knew that much, but for now things could go along relatively smoothly, and she'd deal with the bad stuff when it happened.

Even if the people who knew kept quiet, it would still be obvious from the first episode of *The New Mickey Mouse Club*, when Christina was there in living color. But there was a month to go before that happened. A month during which she could be quite normal again— or at least as normal as she could feel these days. Her secret felt huge inside her. She really wanted to spill it out, but didn't dare.

The days went by, and she settled into the routine of fall. Classes, homework, hanging out with friends, doing stuff with her family. There was the mall, all kinds of things. The weather began to turn cooler. She spent a lot of time in her room, as she'd always done, listening to music and singing, her voice improving all the time from the exercises the vocal coaches had given her.

Then it was October, and the new season of the show began. How should she act when people came up to her?

Nonchalant, as if it had been nothing? Or proud of what she'd done? Maybe a mix of the two.

She was certainly prepared for the worst when she turned up for school after the show had aired, and she wasn't disappointed. Her friends thought it was really cool that she was on television, but wondered why she'd never told them about it. After all, they were supposed to be *friends*, and friends didn't keep secrets from each other, did they? There were kids who looked up to her. And there were other kids who just hated the fact that she'd done something they wanted to do. Those were the ones who could make her life an absolute misery.

It was just like it had been after *Star Search*, although at least this time no one was slashing Shelly's tires. People were ignoring her, even shunning her at school. Others were taunting her. Her friends stuck by her, but even they seemed a little more distant than they used to be. It was weird. Why couldn't they be happy that she'd done something special? She was there representing the school, representing Wexford. There were more articles about her in the local papers, which made kids hate her even more. The whole thing was warped. Christina knew she was the same person she'd always been. She wasn't snooty, wasn't putting on any airs, and everyone was treating her like some kind of outcast.

It had been bad enough when she was eight, but now that she was twelve—almost thirteen—it was much worse. Christina, like all girls at that age, was far more sensitive to being liked or disliked. And this was really getting to her. She was going to school every day, but she no longer wanted to be there; she wanted to be somewhere far, far away where the people weren't mean to her.

Because she was on television every week, the harassment didn't fade away. In fact, it seemed, to get worse, as the kids came to resent what they saw as her fame. In truth, Christina was far from famous. She was just herself, a girl on a television show, doing something she loved. She was as normal as the rest of them, if they'd just let her be and accept her for who she was.

It was an upsetting experience for Christina and Shelly was really concerned about her oldest daughter. Talking to teachers didn't really help; there wasn't a whole lot they could do. It was a problem *at* school, but not really *about* school The teachers couldn't stop the other kids feeling the way they did about Christina.

Finally, Shelly and Christina sat down and talked about it. It was a long discussion, with a lot of tears, and a lot of unhappiness brought to the surface, but it did get everything out in the open. And it was apparent that Christina couldn't continue at her present school, certainly not the way things were—and they didn't seem likely to change. What she needed was a new school. It still wouldn't be a guarantee of everything working out fine, as Shelly pointed out, but if Christina went in new, and was quite up-front about what she did, and the show she was on, it might help.

The conversation made Christina feel a lot better. She knew her mom really cared, as well as the rest of her family, and that they hated to see her this way. But actually doing something about the problem, taking a step in the right direction, cheered her up. It made everything more tolerable. And she could call her friends from the show, and talk to them. A couple of them had endured the same thing, and they could talk about that.

After some searching and interviews with principals, Shelly found a school not too far from home where Christina might well be accepted. Changing schools would be quite traumatic, but Christina was ready for it. After Christmas, right after her birthday, when she was thirteen, she'd start at the new school. Everything would seem fresh and clean then, and she could begin her teenage years in the right way.

It is a major birthday, thirteen. It is when you move from childhood to adolescence, when you *really* start to grow up properly, and things begin to happen—boyfriends and stuff like that. There were cards from her family, from the friends who'd proved themselves to be true, and from members of the show's cast. There were presents, of course: a lot of music, clothes, all the stuff she wanted. And when the new year rang in, it meant that summer wasn't too far away, even if it was snowing outside. And summer would mean a return to Florida.

A new school meant new traumas, but at least they were of a different kind. Christina knew nobody there. She had to find her classes, get to know a whole new set of teachers—the things everyone has to face when they change schools. But this would at least be a new start. Yes she sang, yes she was on television. Sure, there'd be some kids who didn't like it, but it seemed as if the majority accepted her for who she was. Like any school, there were some she didn't want to know and who could have cared less about her. She didn't try and come on like a star, but just like herself. A few recognized her from the show, she got to know some others, and after the initial shock, she found herself feeling more at home there than she ever had at the old place. She could relax and be happy again, which was a feeling she hadn't experienced for a while. It was cool.

One thing that did astonish her about being on the show was the amount of mail that was forwarded to her. She knew people watched it and liked it, but she never expected to be getting real fan mail. Okay, so there weren't sacks and sacks of it every day, but letters now and then, from other kids, people like her, who said they admired her. She read every one, and replied to them, because they were people, like she was.

In the mail one day, however, was a different kind of letter. The note was on a letterhead, and while the writer complimented her voice, he was more than a fan. His name was Steve Kurtz. He'd been impressed by what he'd seen and heard of Christina on television, and wondered if by any chance she had a manager. If she didn't, then it was a job that would interest him. With a manager, she could do a lot more than *The New Mickey Mouse Club*. There would be other opportunities, like performing, and possibly even making her own album.

It wasn't like the idea hadn't occurred to her, but it seemed more like a dream than something that was a possibility. She had lots of CDs, but imagining one with her own name on it seemed . . . unreal. She showed the letter to her mother, and they sat and talked about it. It wouldn't hurt to hear what he had to say, they both agreed, although it was a rule that school came before everything else, especially as Christina was so happy now.

They called Steve Kurtz, and Shelly spent awhile on the phone with him. It would be the first of several calls before he flew out to Pittsburgh to meet the family. He saw the potential in Christina, and believed that, in time, she could become a big star. She had, as many people said, "a big voice," the kind that made people stop and listen, even among the others on the show. He realized that nothing might happen immediately, but he could help develop Christina as a singer, get in contact with people. That way, when she was ready—and when the business was ready for her—things would be a lot easier. The most important thing was that he believed in her and her abilities.

The idea of Christina having a manager was a big step for Shelly. Being on the show was one thing; it took up the summers, and while it made her a professional, it was innocent. A manager implied something more than that. It meant thinking ahead, making some recordings, trying hard to get a record deal. Her girl was only thirteen, and Shelly wasn't sure Christina was ready for all that.

Shelly thought that before she gave her consent the matter required a lot of discussion and thought; after all, since Christina was still young, Shelly was the one who'd have to sign the management contract. She wanted to be certain that Kurtz wouldn't try to rush Christina, and that he'd respect the idea of her getting a good education above all else. Only when she was convinced was she willing to put her name on the dotted line.

There was one thing he wanted to do soon, though, and that was make a tape of Christina singing. It had to be properly recorded, in a studio, with musicians who knew what they were doing. It would be a calling card of sorts, something to send out to record companies so they'd be aware of Christina Aguilera.

Making the tape was a real thrill for Christina, picking the songs she loved and sang best, then going into the studio to sing them. Television had been a great experience, and she'd done some recording then, too, but this was *her* project, a whole tape featuring just her. To be there, at the microphone, with the headphones on so she could hear the backing track, was like a dream come true in itself.

It was a lot of work, running through take after take until she absolutely nailed it, but she didn't mind. She was just happy to be there, to be able to sing with real backup instead of in her room with a hairbrush. This was real, this was what it was all about.

Finally it was done, and she sat in the control booth, listening to herself at loud volume through some clear speakers, and it was hard to believe that was her. She sounded so . . . powerful, so mature. It was a surprise, even to her ears. This was the next step, she understood that. The next step to making it all happen.

Chapter Four

Kurtz sent out the tape to a number of record labels, but while there was some interest in someone who could sing that well, no one was biting yet. Grunge was at the height of its popularity, with all the bands from Seattle and the Seattle wannabes dominating sales. And in its wake, alternative music had taken off too. There were some pop acts who more than held their own—Mariah, Whitney, Boyz II Men—but trying to break in a new singer, especially someone so young, would have been very difficult. There simply didn't seem to be the market at the moment for more artists in the mainstream. Kids of Christina's age hadn't had someone to idolize, really, since New Kids on the Block had broken up—and record executives were not looking for new teen stars. The industry was making money; why try and rock the boat with something new?

None of that helped Christina, but her manager had warned her from the start that she probably wouldn't be getting a record deal in the immediate future, so she wasn't too disappointed by the news. The main thing was that she'd now had real experience in a studio, so when her big chance came, she wouldn't be a total novice. And summer was getting closer every day, time to get back to Florida and have some real fun. Even school had been good since she'd started at the new place. All in all, there was absolutely nothing wrong with her life.

She'd made some new friends, and hung on to a few of the old friends—the real ones, who'd been with her through thick and thin. Her family was there for her, and everything seemed great.

Finally it was time to return to Orlando, with exactly the same routine as the year before—Christina and Shelly would go down, and the rest of the family would join them later, for a vacation. Instead of nerves, this time all Christina felt was anticipation. She was a year older and wiser. She'd been singing constantly at home (and in the studio), so she knew her voice had developed. And she was eager to see all her friends from the previous summer, to see how everyone had changed and grown, to talk, laugh, and perform.

It could easily have been the same apartment they'd had the year before, but Christina wasn't paying much attention. She was too excited, too eager to get to the soundstage. But that was going to have to wait until the following morning. For now she just needed to come down a little, and get a good night's sleep—which was easier said than done. By the time the car picked her up the following morning, Christina was buzzing with joy.

The parents were there too, for an initial meeting, and that was when Disney told everyone that this would be the final season of *The New Mickey Mouse Club*. Like the original, it had run its course. For Christina, it was devastating news. She wasn't sure what she'd imagined, but it was somehow more than just two summers of recording shows. The others, the ones who'd been there much longer than her, were far more distraught. This had been a huge part of their lives. But they were professionals. They might have been sad, but they'd go out with a real bang that people would remember.

"We used to joke about backstage and say, 'When-

ever the show ends, we'll all go off our separate ways
and become stars.' " Christina laughs now. But there
was more than a grain of truth in it all. "We're all so
dedicated and driven, I'm not surprised at any of the
success of my co-Mouseketeers."

They all had something to prove: that the show could
be a very vital thing, not just to them, but to the people
watching, too. Decisions had been made, and the show
had run its course, but if they went out strongly, maybe
at some point it would be revived (and there are petitions
on the Net to bring back the show). Everyone had
changed, of course. Abilities had been sharpened, people
had grown up over the course of the last ten months,
and everyone was cooler than before. But no one was
acting like a star—how could they around the others?
They were all just normal kids who'd come together and
put on a show. Normal kids with special talents who'd
worked very hard to get there.

In a lot of ways, Christina still felt like the newbie,
the baby, but that was okay. The others all loved her. It
didn't take long before she and Britney were as close as
they had been the summer before, hanging together, gos
siping, laughing, special buds on the set.

Everyone pushed themselves harder, knowing it was
going to be the last time they'd do things. Everyone
wanted everything to be perfect. There was a special
feeling about it every day, a true sense of purpose, a
mission about what they were doing there. They loved
it, they all worked well as an ensemble, and they didn't
want it to end, even though they accepted it was going
to.

While there was a sense of finality about everything,
there was also a feeling of new beginnings. They all had
talent, they all had ambition, they'd all go on to do other

things in their special fields, and they'd meet up again—
but this time as big stars. It was the kind of thing people
say, but they all felt it was very real. And they all felt
it could happen.

But even with the dark cloud of ending on the horizon, it wasn't a gloomy summer—in fact, anything but.
They all had fun. They went places together. They
laughed even more than they had the year before. Christina was having the time of her life, with people she
really liked, people who were just like her. It was cool.

The season they taped that summer turned out to be
something very special, something that would live on in
all their hearts, as well as in the memories of all those
who saw it. They sang, acted, and danced their hearts
out. While plenty of them were sure they'd go on to do
other things in the entertainment business, they all knew
how uncertain it was, and that this might be their very
last chance to shine. So shine they did. Every day became a chance to top the day that had gone before, and
Christina joined in the spirit of it. She'd worked hard
over the winter and spring, and was in phenomenal
voice—even the others on the show noticed how much
she'd improved. The vocal coach, in particular, was impressed with her advancement. She was still only thirteen, but sounded so much older. Her grasp of phrasing
was exceptional, and she could hold a note and soar like
very few singers. She was someone with a real future.

Unlike the previous year, this didn't seem like an
endless summer, if only because everyone knew that
when it was over, it would be really over—no thoughts
of coming back the next year. But that didn't stop Christina from having a great vacation when her family arrived, taking her brother and sister places, being goofy
and silly, and introducing her siblings to the other cast

members. In a way, it was even better than last year, because, as the recording ended, the pressure was off. They didn't have to wonder if they'd done well enough to be invited back. This was it. It was just *fun*, doing things for sheer pleasure.

Of course, Christina had always sung for the joy of it, so this was nothing new to her, but it was still so cool to be doing it with people who thought exactly like her, people with their own talents, that complemented her own.

Still, there was a question at the back of her mind— where could she go after this? What could she do? She was a singer, but she was thirteen. None of the record companies were interested. Unless someone came up with another TV show like *The New Mickey Mouse Club*, there was no real opportunity in that direction. Was it a case of going home and just singing in her bedroom again, waiting for some lucky break? She began to wonder whether, for every step forward, there wasn't another one back, and whether fate was really against her.

These were perfectly natural thoughts, and all the other cast members had them too. The show had been great, but how could they make it into something more? They'd all had a taste of real performing, and loved it— but what would they do afterwards? It wasn't going to be easy.

Then again, show business is rarely easy. You need talent, but you also need luck and the right break to make it big. Those three things rarely come together. These days, a lot of marketing can help, but all the push in the world isn't going to make it happen if it's not what the public wants to hear or see. The bottom line is being in the right place at the right time, and knowing the right people. The problem is, there's no knowing what is the right place, or when is the right time. That's the luck factor.

So, for all that they swore they'd all be famous, the cast of *The New Mickey Mouse Club* didn't really know if they'd ever see each other again, and that made their farewells very difficult and tearful. Working together so intensely, they'd become close friends. They'd helped each other, listened to each other's secrets and crushes.

Driving to the airport, it was hard for Christina to believe she wouldn't be back there the following summer. There was a little part of her that hoped the Disney people would change their minds, that maybe they hadn't been totally serious about ending the show.

Back home in Wexford, she knew that it was over. Apart from school, what was there to look forward to? Friends, family—but they'd be there anyway. It was back to a very dull routine of studying, books, singing in her room. It would pass, when she got used to it all again. But nothing would be the same. She loved the excitement of performing, of entertaining, of singing for people.

Christina talked to her manager, and told him how she felt. He counseled patience. He knew just how great her voice was, and he realized that other people would come to that conclusion. But at thirteen, Christina had a lot of time ahead of her in which to make it. There was nothing wrong with enjoying just being a kid while she could; if she missed all that now, she'd just regret it later. It echoed what her mother told her. You make the most of what you've got, you enjoy it to the fullest while it's there.

It was a time for listening to the blues, for hearing Etta James wail, and wallowing in it. But the simple fact was that Christina had already achieved far more than most girls even dreamed of. She was driven, that was understood, but even the most driven people sometimes have to spend a little time in neutral. She'd come a long way because of her talent. She knew she could go all the way, but as everyone kept telling her, it was a journey to be made in stages, not all at once. So she did her best to hang back and wait, not to seem too frustrated, to listen and to continue to learn from everything she heard, and to discover more and more about music. For now, really, that was all she could do.

One of the beauties of life, though, is that you never know quite what's going to happen. Just when the future seems certain, something will turn up to change everything. As far as Christina was concerned, the next few years looked to be an unending vista of school and Wexford; it was unlikely there would be too many thrills along the way.

But her manager continued to work on her behalf. The fact that American record companies weren't interested limited his options, but he knew there had to be more possibilities out there. After all, America wasn't the only country in the world, and there had to be places where they appreciated a really good singer, even if she didn't fit in to an obvious niche.

One of the biggest markets for music was Japan. Westerners whose names meant little at home could become big stars there, and artists whose popularity had all but vanished elsewhere could command big audiences (and big money) there. Singers who would never dream of making television ads in their native countries made them in Japan. In that regard, it was a very strange place, with a seemingly huge appetite for Western music of all kinds. But would they be open to a girl no one had ever heard of? That was what Steve Kurtz needed to know.

If he didn't try, he'd never know, so he used his Japanese contacts to feel out the idea, without ever telling Christina—there was no point in raising her hopes unless he knew something for certain. It was a long shot, he knew, but if it paid off, who knew where it might lead?

Kurtz's contacts obviously knew the Japanese market well, because they put him in touch with the manager of Keizo Nakanishi, who, while unknown in America, was a real pop star in Japan, the kind of artist who always seemed to be on the charts. What he was looking to do was record a duet with an American female singer, someone who sang like Mariah or Whitney. The problem was finding someone like that, since neither of those two seemed likely to get in the duet business anytime soon. If Christina had a voice like that, Nakanishi's manager said, then there might well be something to talk about.

The faxes continued to fly back and forth, and Kurtz sent over Christina's demo tape. He knew it was good, and he could truthfully add that her voice had improved a lot since then. At first he didn't hear anything, and he feared they'd been rejected, maybe because of Christina's age. But finally there was an enthusiastic response—Keizo was eager to do a duet with Christina. It was time to pass on the word to his artist.

Christina had never heard of Keizo, but, as Kurtz pointed out, he'd never heard of her before, either. This was going to be a pretty major deal. In all likelihood, she was going to have a hit in Japan, and who knew what that might turn into? She could get a record deal there, maybe do some television, possibly even tour—who knew?

All of a sudden, Christina felt excited about life again!

And why shouldn't she, with something as big as this around the corner? Working with an established star was a great way to introduce her to the Japanese market, and the way it worked, she was set not only to sing on the single, but also to appear in the video—all tremendous exposure.

The song selected—by Keizo's management—was called "All I Wanna Do." It didn't exactly stretch Christina's vocal ability, but that wasn't the name of this particular game. She wasn't the star of this song, merely a foil to Keizo. But if it did well—and given his stature in Japanese pop, that seemed very likely—it could lead to much bigger things.

One thing it didn't mean, at least not immediately, was a trip to Japan. Given technology, it was quite possible for almost everything to be recorded first, then a tape sent to America for Christina to add her part. She'd heard the song and the arrangement, and knew exactly what was required of her. She'd spent a lot of time rehearsing, getting every note, every phrase and nuance perfect, so she was ready when the call came to go to the studio. There wasn't even a need to fly to L.A. or New York for her vocal. A good studio in Pittsburgh had everything she needed, so one Saturday Shelly drove her down, and she spent the morning recording take after take. She knew she'd nailed it early on, but it was a case of give them everything, lots of choices. The final decision was out of her hands.

After that, as always, it was a case of sit back and wait until she received the finished product in the mail from Japan. That was a real thrill, to know this was going to be a single, and that her name would be on it, even if it was in small letters in a language she couldn't read. It was her, on disc!

There was still the little matter of the video, and for that she did have to fly to Japan. Over spring break, she and Shelly boarded a jet to the West Coast, then another heading across the Pacific to the Land of the Rising Sun. It was first-class all the way—no half measures by the Japanese record company. And once they landed in Tokyo, where everything seemed both familiar and alien, it was all business.

The shoot was booked for the next day, and from her experience in television, Christina knew it was going to be a long grind, that most of the time would be spent setting up shots, rather than actually filming. But that was okay. She was here, hearing her voice on the playback, and working with someone who was a major Japanese star. How many fourteen-year-olds had that kind of luck?

It was very different from taping the show, though, far more intense and exhausting. After an early start, it was late, already dark, by the time Christina and her mom were ferried back to their hotel. But there were at least a few more days when they could play tourist, and go around buying souvenirs to take home to the rest of the family, and for Christina to give her friends at school, if only to prove she'd really been there.

The record was scheduled for a release later in the spring, and if it did well, there was already talk of a tour for Keizo. But what would that mean for Christina? She was about to find out.

Holding the cassette of the song had been incredible, but it didn't even compare to having copies of the fin-

At the Teen Choice Awards.

(© Steve Granitz/Retna Ltd.)

Happiness is a Number One single.

(© Leo Sorel/Retna Limited, USA)

Close up.

(© Walter McBride/Retna Limited, USA)

Chillin' in Disney World.

(© Walter McBride/Retna Limited, USA)

How to look hot.

(© Steve Granitz/Retna Ltd.)

At the MTV Video Music Awards.

(© Bill Davila/Retna Limited, USA)

Christina posing with Tommy Lee at the MTV Video Music Awards.

(© Bill Davila/Retna Limited, USA)

Everybody's got questions for Christina.

In concert.
(© Steve Granitz/Retna Ltd.)

In concert.
(© Steve Granitz/Retna Ltd.)

ished disc, the one that would be released. That really *was* a dream come true. She played it over and over, if only to make sure it was real, and not something she'd imagined. She was so proud and thrilled it was impossible not to keep smiling, so hard that her face almost ached. This was what it felt like now—how would it be when she had her *own* record?

Her manager kept her informed on the record's sales in Japan, and, to her amazement, Christina was suddenly a performer on a hit single! It was the kind of thing that only happened in fairy tales, but it was here, and now, and it truly involved her. She pinched herself, and it was still there. The best news of all was that they wanted her to tour Japan with Keizo and sing the duet with him. Her career really was beginning to move ahead after all. Maybe not in America, but you had to start somewhere, and she was more than happy to take this. Dates were set up for her summer vacation, and then Steve Kurtz came up with an even bigger surprise: on the strength of the hit and her involvement with *The New Mickey Mouse Club*, he'd managed to land her a spot on the Golden Stag Festival. It would only be two songs, but that was better than nothing. And it was going to be somewhere she'd never been before—in Romania, specifically in Transylvania. She'd be appearing on the same bill as Diana Ross and Sheryl Crow, which wasn't a bad deal at all.

Christina was stunned—who wouldn't be? First, at the place—she didn't know Transylvania really existed outside horror movies—then at the thought of actually performing on a stage, alone, for a crowd. It was the kind of thing she'd imagined when she was singing in her room, but to know it was going to happen was . . .

well, exciting and scary. Her summers seemed to be getting better and better every year.

Flying back to Japan, knowing that she was going to be onstage, was amazing. It was a long flight, but she savored every second of it, unable to get to sleep for the excitement racing through her. If this was what she felt like now, how would it be when she was there, with the music playing and the audience listening?

Well, she'd find out soon enough. But first there were rehearsals. She'd never sung "All I Wanna Do" with a live band before—or even with Keizo, for that matter. But Christina was a seasoned professional by now, one who knew exactly what to do, and who took direction well. Her training had been good. She would only appear for the duet, and that would be her sole contribution to the evening, but that was fine; it didn't matter. She was here, she was going to be singing. And this was a good way to ease into live performance.

It didn't stop her from feeling incredibly nervous before the opening show, but as soon as the first chords of the song began, that all disappeared, and she was ready to walk on and do her part. Which she did, superbly, never missing a note or a beat, holding herself well, and getting an amazing rush of energy from all the people who'd come out to see Keizo. Maybe someday they'd be coming to see her. . . .

There were a number of shows on the Japanese tour, and each was better than the last for Christina. There were plenty of other thrills, too, like seeing the country, riding the bullet train between cities, and experiencing a foreign culture. It wasn't too difficult for her to envision doing this kind of thing for a living someday.

Of course, she had to remember that this was just a summer, and that in September she'd be back in school.

But it was the best summer ever, and it wasn't over yet.

The knowledge that she'd be singing alone in Romania kept her on edge. But at least her debut on the stage had been easy and straightforward. For her solo show, though, she had backing tapes, and she'd rehearse with them endless times. The only things that could go wrong were technical problems or if she got stage fright, and the latter seemed unlikely. Being up there, she realized, she was in her element. It all felt perfectly natural.

Going straight from Japan to Romania was severe culture shock, from a land of plenty to a poor country, one that was recognizable but still very, very different. The amenities were lacking, although all the festival performers were housed in good hotels and looked after in the best possible manner. But it was impossible not to see the deprivation of the people who lived there and feel for them. All she could hope was that the festival would bring a little light into their lives for a few days.

It was by far the biggest audience she'd ever seen—bigger even than the concerts in Japan. There were *ten thousand* people out there waiting to hear her, and that was more than a bit daunting. She thought she was past stage fright, but it couldn't help giving her some butterflies inside her stomach. She was a pro, though, and this was what she did. The music began, she had the microphone in her hand, and she charged out on the stage.

Immediately, it was a buzz like no other, the cheering just for her, so loud she could barely hear herself in the monitors. She was singing, but the crowd was overwhelming, and it just energized her. She sang her heart out on the first song for them, and the applause was just wild—and this for someone the audience had never even heard of. They loved her, and they loved her for her music, not because she was a star.

The best way to repay them, Christina thought, and to make sure they remembered her, was to go to them. So, as her second and last song began, she climbed off the stage and into the audience, singing to them while she was among them.

It caused a sensation among the Romanians. They certainly hadn't been expecting this, but they reveled in it. Everyone, it seemed, wanted to get close to her, to touch her, to see her. What she'd thought might be a nice little walk in the crowd seemed to be rapidly turning into a riot! For her own safety, as well as for all the people closing in, she did the only thing she could—she climbed back onto the stage to finish the song.

The applause was deafening. No one had expected her to act like that, to break down the wall between performer and audience that way, to be not a star, but one of the people, and it was really appreciated, especially since it probably wouldn't be that way with any of the other acts (neither Sheryl Crow nor Diana Ross was likely to get down from the stage). Perhaps Christina could get away with it because she was unknown, but it left an indelible impression on everyone who'd seen her. All of a sudden, she was a star in Transylvania. And that was better than not being a star anywhere. A lot better.

She walked off the stage exhausted, but grinning widely. It had been an incredible kick to do that, although it didn't sink in until later just how dangerous it had been. Anything could have happened to her down there, and she'd have been powerless to stop it. But in the end she'd been safe. Shelly wasn't happy with it all, but Christina hadn't come down from performing yet. It was amazing.

From Romania, it was home again, making her summer into a genuine around-the-world trip, the kind of thing that usually only happens in stories. But it was real, and she had the pictures to prove it. Now this was going to be something to tell them about at school.

Chapter Five

And the fact that she would be telling them at school was part of the problem. How did you make the adjustment from what she'd just done to being a regular kid again? From playing concerts to studying for a test? How could a trip to the mall compare to singing to thousands of people?

It certainly wasn't a question a lot of girls had to answer, and Christina didn't know exactly what to do about it. Settling back into a routine was going to take awhile, and in the meantime it was impossible not to feel unsettled and somehow dissatisfied.

But, as her mother had told her, education always came first. There could be no other way at all. And good grades were more important than anything else.

So Christina buckled down to her schoolwork, and spent her free time with her friends and family. After she'd told them about everything, it was as if she had nothing more to say for a while. She kept looking at the photos, reliving it all, and wanting to do it again. But that all depended on circumstances. Her manager had hoped for some kind of record deal in Japan, but that didn't seem to be happening. A hit as part of a duo overseas didn't seem to carry any weight with American record labels. Her resume looked great, but there was nothing happening *now*, and now was when she wanted things to be happening. It was frustrating for her.

Gradually, though, the feelings lessened, and normality returned. There were more immediate concerns to be addressed, like learning chapter seven in her social studies book, or figuring out the math problems she had for homework. That was life, as her mother pointed out. It had its highs and it had its flat spots—and for most people, there were a lot more flat spots than highs. Besides, Christina had always wanted to be treated like a normal kid, hadn't she? Well, that was what was happening.

Nothing in her career sparkled on the horizon. The school year passed by slowly. There were boys, and friends, and there was fun, too. Life did take on plenty of color, and she had to admit that dating was enjoyable, in a new way.

Of course, she didn't stop singing. There were still plenty of hours in her bedroom practicing. Even if it was just scales, she loved it, pushing herself a little further, making her voice into an instrument that was even more supple than it had been before. She could hear how it was developing, and she was learning more about the technical side, too, reading music, listening, understanding techniques that would help her improve. She didn't want to be a diva, just someone making the very most of her gift, even if her career did seem to go in fits and starts.

But that was okay, as both her mother and her manager told her. Her career was gaining momentum slowly, and it would all happen for her when the time was right. She was still young, and had plenty of years ahead of her in which to be a star. There was no rush, and no pressure to succeed. It was better to let everything develop at its own pace. Soon enough she'd have schedules, recording dates, videos, and stylists to worry about, and then she'd sometimes wish she was away from it all. For now it was better to enjoy just being a girl, without too many cares beyond passing the next test, and let the world happen.

They said it often, and Christina did listen. It was true, there were things she enjoyed, and there were the challenges of school to occupy her mind. She had a set of friends she really loved, and high school was proving to be a better experience than middle school. All in all, there was absolutely nothing wrong with her life, and they were right, it was far from over yet. More than that, the best things were still to come. Everyone could have been telling her that just to make her feel better, but she really believed it; things were going to happen for her.

So she settled down. She didn't forget about everything that had happened—how could she?—but she did put it in a different box in her mind, and concentrated on the things at hand, while never losing the focus of her singing. After so many years at the center of her life, it wasn't going to budge for anything, and she didn't want it to. When she was alone it was a comfort and a joy to be able to open her mouth and hear the melodies come out. It was fun to challenge herself with an Etta James song or a jazz standard, just to see how well she could do against someone who could really sing. Or to try to be as funky as Chaka Khan, to see if she could climb as high as Mariah. Every time she pushed herself just a tiny bit further.

By now she had confidence in her voice. It was still growing, although it was a big voice already. At home she didn't dare go for full volume; it was simply too loud. And if someone saw her singing, they always found it hard to believe that that could come out of such a little girl, which made her smile. You didn't have to be large to have a large voice. And she could sing passionately, too; she could still get into the heart of a song and make it completely hers. Even more than her voice, she sometimes thought that was her real gift.

When summer rolled around, and she wasn't going to Florida, or traveling abroad, the time away from school seemed very long and very empty. There was still stuff to do, but it just wasn't the same anymore. Still, that was the way it went. Before she'd been involved with *The New Mickey Mouse Club* she'd managed to fill her time. Granted, she'd just been a kid then, but if she looked around, there'd be plenty to do. Still, nothing beat performing, and she just hoped there would come a time soon when she'd be able to do it again.

She hung out with her best friend, Marcy. They went to the mall, went everywhere they could think of. There was time with her brother and sisters, with her mom, and lots of time practicing. The weather was good, but it was hard to feel satisfied. When she had time on her hands, it was all too easy for the memories to come flooding back, and they did, like the feeling that had gone through her as she jumped into the crowd at the Golden Stag Festival.

She talked to her manager regularly, and he kept her spirits up, telling her about the things he was trying to fix up for her, and reminding her that her time would come. Okay, so it wouldn't be this summer, so she should just relax and see what was going to happen the following year. You never knew, after all. . . .

She never knew, but she continually hoped. Christina's manager continued to try the record companies. He had her go into the studio and record a new demo tape, to illustrate just how much her voice had improved in the last couple of years, and the resume that accompanied it looked very impressive for a teenager.

Perhaps even more important, there was another change happening, this time in popular music itself. Alternative was going out of style. Bands like the Spice Girls—who'd been huge everywhere else in the world—were showing that even America had an appetite for good, breezy pop music, and for girls who could be teen idols and role models for other girls. In their wake came a lot of groups, some of whom, like the Backstreet Boys, had already proved their popularity overseas. Suddenly the United States was marching to a pop beat, in a way it hadn't since the early '70s. And that meant the record labels were looking for younger artists, even largely unproven ones, who could reach a teen and prepubescent audience.

Obviously, Steve Kurtz had been watching that trend very carefully on behalf of his artist. He could sense that her time was coming. But there was a difference between bands and solo artists, particularly young female solo artists. The country wasn't ready for Christina yet, but it was getting closer and closer. That was why the new demo helped. It reminded people that she existed, and that she could really sing, not just pop music, but anything, that she was an artist who could have real longevity.

At RCA Records, A&R (Artist and Repertoire—the department responsible for signing new acts) director Ron Fair remembered Christina's first tape. It had been impressive for someone so young, but this new one was leaps and bounds ahead. And he could see the way the market was heading. The interest in teen culture—not just music, but movies and television too, along with a proliferation of magazines—was growing every day. He was already certain that the next big boy band would be 'N Sync, which included two alumni of *The New Mickey Mouse Club*, Christina's former colleagues JC and Justin.

But he also knew the market wasn't ready for a solo girl singer yet, even someone as good as Christina. If anyone released a record by her now, it would simply sink, unheard, and that would be the end of things. He agreed with her manager that the girl could have a long and fruitful career. A voice that needed special nurturing.

"She was fearless," he recalls. "She had perfect intonation and command of her instrument that normally you would see in someone a lot older. I was struck by her amazing voice, her budding beauty, and I decided to take a shot and sign her to a demo deal."

That news, when it came through, was simply electrifying. Her manager was careful to point out to Christina that it didn't automatically mean a record deal, but she was over the moon. This was exactly what she'd been working toward for years. Some record company had finally thought she was good enough to let her record. Being "in development" really wasn't the same as a full record deal. It meant that the company would help her, and work with her, with the chance to sign her if they liked the result. But to Christina those were merely details. Everything was going to work out, she had no doubt of that.

Suddenly her world seemed alive again, and full of endless possibilities. How could it be anything else now? Since she was under eighteen (she'd actually just turned seventeen), it was Shelly who put her name on the contract, but that didn't matter to Christina. This was her very first step in the future she'd been dreaming about.

The first steps are often the smallest, however. A development deal didn't mean she was going to be whisked off to a studio and treated like a queen. It meant that for a while nothing would happen at all, unless she was very lucky. But as people kept telling her, you never knew what was going to be around the next corner.

Ron Fair was pleased with his new signing, and planned on keeping a close eye on her. There was every chance that she could become another Mariah Carey, someone who could grow as an artist, and keep an audience with her. What he really needed was some way to introduce her to the American public, some way that didn't consist of a new album and new single. Something to prime people for that, as it were.

He was still thinking about it when his phone rang. It was the nature of the music business for him to know a lot of people, so when the call turned out to be a friend of his from Disney who worked in the soundtrack department, he was happy to talk.

As it turned out, he was especially happy to talk to this man. Disney was preparing to release a new animated feature, *Mulan*, and they were working on the soundtrack. They had the songs, but they were currently looking for singers. In particular, they needed someone young, someone with a stunning voice and strong range, to sing a ballad. Did Fair know of anyone they could audition?

As it happened, he certainly did have someone in mind. . . .

He called Steve Kurtz, who immediately jumped on the phone to Disney. They needed someone who could handle a ballad, sing it with some real meaning, and who could reach some pretty high notes with assurance. That, he told them, completely described Christina. He offered to send them her studio demo, but they wanted to know exactly how she sounded *now*, and they needed it in a couple of days. That ruled out getting her into the studio.

Kurtz called Christina, and told her what he wanted her to do. He knew she had some karaoke tapes, the type that provide a backing track but no vocals. He wanted her to select one, one that would show what she could do, and tape it. It could be a really rough tape, as long as her singing came across strongly. She needed to do it right then, and overnight it to the people at Disney. While she wasn't a shoo-in, he honestly believed that once they heard her, they'd be as convinced by her talent as he was.

The question, as always, was what song she should sing. She looked through her tapes, and decided on one that seemed perfect—Whitney Houston's "I Wanna Run To You." She could inject some real power into it, and it showed how well she could handle the high notes.

After that, it was just a matter of setting up two cassette recorders, and finding a place in her living room to stand and sing where she could get a good balance between the tape and her voice, so one wasn't completely drowning out the other. That took a little while. Once she'd accomplished that, all that remained was the best possible take of the song, one that satisfied her. Her standards were high, particularly for her own performances, since she knew exactly what she was capable of, and wanted to show herself in the best possible light. But there was also a time factor. The tape needed to go off that day. The pressure was on.

It didn't take long for her to nail it to her satisfaction, as well as she'd ever sung the song. She played it back, smiling, then rewound the tape, and Shelly drove her to a place where she could overnight it to Disney. It was going to be fine, she could feel it.

Sleep wasn't easy. This was something where there would be an immediate decision.

And indeed there was. As soon as the Disney executives heard Christina's tape, they were on the phone to her manager. They wanted her for the soundtrack. The fact that she'd worked with Disney in the past, on *The New Mickey Mouse Club*, didn't carry any weight; that was then, and this was now. They not only wanted her, they wanted her out in Los Angeles as soon as possible to record. They needed someone, according to Christina, who could hit "high E above middle C," which was easily in her range, as she'd demonstrated on her tape.

People at Disney were already arranging travel for Christina and her mom from Pittsburgh to Los Angeles. She had to leave the next day. It meant time off school, but these were exceptional circumstances, and Shelly was willing to make allowances. Disney, after all, wasn't just a company, it was an American institution. And she fully understood just what kind of break this could be for her daughter. Besides, it was just going to be a very quick trip there and back, long enough for her to record one song and that was all.

It was a hastily arranged trip, and Christina was nervous. A lot was resting on her abilities here. She had to adapt herself to the song, not the song to her. She had to deliver the kind of performance they wanted, do it right, and do it quickly. She knew she could, but it didn't make the pressure any less.

The recording studio was more advanced than any studio she'd been in before, a real state-of-the-art facility. That was unnerving, too. It almost seemed more like a computer lab than a place where music was made. She was jet-lagged and nervous. She hadn't slept well. And she had to give the performance of a lifetime.

First she was played the song, with a rough vocal that seemed pretty good to her. But the real challenge was hitting that high E, which she now calls "the note that changed my life."

Then there was a run-through. Her voice was still cold, but going through the song twice warmed it up, and as she became more familiar with the melody, she captured it and made it her own.

"The song's theme—the struggle to establish your identity—was something I could really relate to as a teenage girl myself," she explains.

She was able to lose herself in it, through take after take, until everyone was satisfied that she'd really gotten it, and what they had on tape was perfect.

"I was ecstatic," Christina says. "These things only come along once every few years. They took a huge chance using an unknown like me."

Any new Disney feature was guaranteed a lot of press, but *Mulan*, an animated feature about a girl who became a warrior in ancient China, was going to be the centerpiece of the year for the company, which made it a very big deal indeed. A lot of people would see it, and hear the music (all of which had been specially written for the film). And plenty of them would go out and buy the soundtrack album—all of which meant many, many people would be hearing Christina. Written by Matthew Wilder (who'd had some chart success in the '80s) and David Zippel, and produced and arranged by Wilder, "Reflection" was the movie's big ballad. It could easily have been written just for Christina, given the emotion she was able to put into it.

When the film was released in June, right after school

ended for the year, Christina was going to be quite famous. Even if her face wasn't everywhere, her voice
would become quite recognizable.

One person who'd been keeping a very close eye on
what happened at Disney was Ron Fair at RCA. He was
overjoyed that Christina had sung on the soundtrack, and
it made him think that perhaps he was being too cau-
tious, simply having Christina in a development deal.
Something like this was going to make a world of difference to her career, and give her a boost no amount
of money or publicity could buy. And with the way the
teen market was growing by leaps and bounds, the country might well be ready for a record by Christina very
soon. Perhaps he really should just sign her to a full
contract.

Christina had just arrived home, exhausted, still a bit
hoarse from flying and having sung so much, when the
phone rang. It was Steve Kurtz, and Christina assumed
he was just checking in, making sure she'd got home
safely. Certainly that was a part of it. He'd been in touch
with the Disney people, who were very happy with her
work. But there was far more. RCA wanted her to do a
record. Forget the development deal, this was the real
thing: her own record contract. It took a second to reg-
ister, and then she was screaming. This was amazing.
This was the very best week of her life, even if everything was happening too fast for her to really process.
Her life had changed completely within the space of five
days. Everything she'd dreamed about and hoped for
was coming together all at once. It was like magic.

Chapter Six

Christina was now officially an RCA recording artist. There was a major thrill in simply saying it and hearing the words. But no one was about to rush an album out to capitalize on her appearance on the *Mulan* soundtrack. There was no hurry. The label was going to do it right, and that meant taking their time, working with Christina to select the right songs. They were going to make sure she got the debut she deserved.

All that was going to take time, and a lot of effort, particularly during what was called the preproduction phase. But once Christina became fully involved, it was going to demand a lot from her. And that meant something would have to give. Shelly sat down with Christina's manager and people from the label, and it was agreed that Christina would finish her junior year at school, and then be tutored for her senior year. At first Shelly wasn't sure; she'd always insisted that school had to come first. But the label promised extensive tutoring—she wouldn't miss out on a thing, and might even end up with a better education. Christina had a chance to realize the dream that had been with her for almost ten years; who was she to stand in the way of that? More than that, she wanted her daughter—all her children—to succeed.

Nothing, however, would happen until the summer, and even then Christina would be concentrating on helping to promote *Mulan* by making some personal appearances. So she still had a few months of "real" school to endure. Although she was eager to move on, now things were happening so fast, it wasn't too bad. She had her friends, and an extra incentive to do well—the more she did this year, the easier home schooling would be for her senior year.

Her family was so proud of her. She'd achieved a great deal, she'd already done things very few people got to do, and she'd barely even scratched the surface of a career yet. And no longer was she just hoping for things to push ahead. She already knew they were; she could simply relax for right now, and concentrate on enjoying herself before the real work began.

To be able to chill a bit like that was peaceful. The only pressure was schoolwork, and she found herself eager to work at that, to get the best grades she could, and prove that she really was a good student—to end her career in high school on a high note.

One thing that didn't worry her was the idea that she might be plunging into all this too young, as a few people thought. While the entertainment industry could chew people up and spit them out, Christina knew she had enough experience to handle herself well.

"I'd be worried about being messed up if I *didn't* do this," she told a reporter. And it was true. Her life was opening up ahead of her, and it would all begin in June, with the premiere of *Mulan* and the end of school.

Mulan, as everyone had predicted, was an immediate smash hit at the box office. There were the usual commercial tie-ins, of course, with toys and books available in stores, and small toys in meals at fast food restaurants. It was a blitz, but that was the way the movie industry seemed to work these days. The movie was quite memorable on its own account, but the excellent songs on the soundtrack hammered it all home.

It wasn't uncommon to release one song from a soundtrack album as a single—Celine Dion's "My Heart Will Go On" from *Titanic* was a prime example, which topped the charts and probably helped the movie (not that it really needed any help)—but it was unusual to make the single a ballad by an unknown artist. That was what Disney did with "Reflection," though, and it immediately thrust Christina front and center into the spotlight. There were promotional appearances to make, specifically on television, where she got to sing the song live on both *CBS This Morning* and *Donny and Marie*—both places which tended to target family audiences, ideal for the movie. Perhaps the biggest thrill, however, was to watch the song climb the Adult Contemporary chart, all the way into the top fifteen. That didn't make it a major hit single, and she wasn't challenging Celine or Mariah or Whitney yet, but it was a hit on her first attempt, which was a definite achievement.

The exposure she was receiving was fantastic, and at least some of the people watching and listening would remember her name when her own record did appear. For now, she was more than happy to concentrate on pushing "Reflection." It was a beautiful song, and one she was not only proud of, but could easily relate to. When it received a Golden Globe nomination for Best Original Song in a Motion Picture, she couldn't have been happier if she'd written it herself. It all reflected well on her, and although it didn't win, simply to have gotten that far was remarkable.

Appearing on television again was a major buzz. June was a busy month for Christina; the single continued to

do well into July (as did the film), and the demand for
her to appear on television, radio, and in person continued. She knew it would taper off soon, but she honestly
didn't mind. Once all this was over, she could begin to
concentrate on her own album, which was something she
was becoming more and more eager to do. Singing for
people and for cameras was wonderful, but it just fired
her desire to be back in the studio, giving a song her
all. Without any shadow of a doubt, she knew she was
ready to do this.

By August, she was free to begin work. And that
meant some *very* major changes in her life. For a start,
she had to leave Pittsburgh. At seventeen, she would be
breaking ties with her family, and moving out to the
West Coast. She'd be back often, and Shelly would be
coming to visit her too, but it was a huge step. It wasn't
even as if she'd been unhappy at home; far from it. But
that was the way it had to be. The recording studios were
in and around Los Angeles, and that was where Christina
needed to be. Shelly and Jim and the kids had their own
settled lives in Wexford.

It wasn't as if Christina would suddenly be thrown
out on her own. She'd be living with a family lined up
by the label, so it would be like home, but with different
people. And she'd be working so hard for the next few
months that she'd hardly have a life anyway. Between
music and her studies, there'd be very little free time
available to her.

The first thing was to come up with a shortlist of
songs for the album. She'd record more than she needed,
but some could be used for B-sides, and others simply
wouldn't make the grade. Ron Fair, the man who'd
signed her and helped her connect with Disney, would
be the executive producer of the project, and he'd be the

one making the final decisions. As was often the case in modern music, there'd be no one producer for the whole album, but different producers and writers would handle individual tracks. It meant a more varied sound and different textures for the record, which would be a mix of more up-tempo dance material and the ballads that were really Christina's long suit.

Having people send material was no problem. There was a wealth of songwriters out there, some established, some not. One of the heaviest hitters among the writers was Diane Warren, who'd been penning hits in many different fields for a long time. She submitted a ballad called "I Turn to You" which Fair immediately knew was perfect for Christina. There was little doubt that it would end up on the finished record, and the same applied to "Reflection," which would be quickly recognizable to anyone who'd seen *Mulan.* Often the writers would also be the producers, especially in the dance-oriented material, which made things easier. But finding sympathetic producers was easier than finding really good songs.

And Fair was well aware of his signing's potential to be huge, not just for a couple of hits, but for many years to come. "She's our Streisand," he says, referring to the world-famous singer, whose career has lasted well over three decades. The label was all in favor of Christina expanding her horizons in every direction, from TV to Broadway to the concert stage. Anything and everything was possible for her. But first, there would be the small matter of a record.

Settling in L.A. was easy, even though it was a strange town. To Christina it seemed permanently covered in a haze of smog, dry and blindingly sunny, and very different from Wexford. She'd brought some of

her stuff with her from home: the important things—
pictures, her favorite CDs, some clothes. It wasn't as if
she were moving out here forever. Once the record was
complete, she'd be back in Pennsylvania again, at least
until it came out.

RCA gave her a couple of days to settle in to her new
digs, and then it was time to get to work. She was there
for the song selection, saying not only whether she liked
something, but why, and what she thought she could do
with it. Christina wasn't treated like a disposable singer,
but a real person, an adult whose opinion mattered—and
she valued that.

The songs' arrangements were formulated to showcase her voice, which would be front and center through-
out the record. Like every singer, her voice was better
in some keys than in others, so sometimes songs would
have to be transposed to suit her—but that was par for
the course with any singer.

When she wasn't at the studios or the offices of RCA,
she was being tutored in a way that made high school
seem relaxed. It was a *very* small class, and Christina
was getting the kind of attention she'd never had in regular school. She was being pushed and challenged—and
she liked it. There were no distractions from learning
when she was there, no one cutting up or distracting the
teacher. Instead, they were getting through the lessons
briskly, and she felt like she was really learning things.

Los Angeles was quickly becoming a very heady experience. There was a ton of new music to discover on
the radio, things she never got to hear at home. She got
interested in a band that was new to her—Limp Bizkit
(although she learned they weren't exactly newcomers).
It was a mixture of rock and hip-hop, and everything
about them, especially the sound of singer Fred Durst,

appealed to a different, wilder side of her. It was about as far as possible from the music she was making, but she liked it anyway. She knew she was going to be marketed as a pop artist, which was perfectly cool, at least for now, but that didn't mean her own tastes were limited to pop. At night, after a long day, the best thing to relax her in her room was to play a B. B. King CD and vanish into the sound of his remarkable, restrained blues guitar. It wasn't pop, but it was very, very real, and it took her outside of herself, away from whatever was going on in her life. As the great jazz musician Duke Ellington had once said, there were only two types of music—good and bad.

And she still had her love of show tunes—this was, after all, the girl who'd learned every song on the *Sound of Music* soundtrack (which might have been why RCA saw Broadway as a possible move in her future). For Christina, music was all-encompassing. From dance beats to ballads to hip-hop to show music, she was in love with it, as long as it was good.

With current studio technology, almost anyone can be made to sound good, even if they can barely carry a tune in a bucket. For someone like Christina, who not only had wonderful pitch, but also a remarkably loud voice (a few people have compared her volume to the late and legendary Ethel Merman, who was perhaps best known for her version of "There's No Business Like Show Business"), the studio with all its gimmicks and gadgets could be a little confining. Christina didn't need her voice tweaked and altered to sound right, as the producers quickly learned. It was fine just the way it came out of her mouth.

At the same time, Christina wasn't criticizing anything. She was being allowed to make this record, and she knew exactly how fortunate she was, and how many other girls would love to be in her shoes. But obviously she wanted it to represent who *she* was, and not be something concocted purely to be a hit. That was why she'd valued being able to give her input on the choice of songs.

Different producers had different favorite studios, and so Christina found herself moving around L.A. to work on different tracks. It wasn't easy to keep it all straight until she walked in and saw a friendly face. And she was learning just how much work was involved in putting each track together. Arrangements were made from the demo versions. If the drum track was computerized, then it had to be programmed, along with whatever other instruments might be sampled. Where live musicians were used, they had to run down their tracks, which meant, first of all, getting the right sound—a process which could take hours of slight adjustments until the producer and engineer were happy. And there were always changes to be made, new ideas brought to the table, things to be added or subtracted, occasionally even a completely new approach to the song, which necessitated a return to square one.

No one said it was easy, and no one said it would be fast. Christina's assumption was that the label would want her record out quickly, so they could capitalize on the celebrity she'd acquired in singing on *Mulan*, but that wasn't the case. They were going to do this right, take their time, and present her properly as an artist—something she greatly valued, rather than being attached to purely one song, although it had been agreed that "Reflection" would appear on her album. And she did love the song; it was a great ballad, and an excellent showcase for her voice.

While the ballads played to her vocal strengths, the whole album couldn't be slow. There had to be a mix of material. And show tunes weren't going to work. She was seventeen, and the people who'd be buying her record would be her age and younger; they needed something faster and danceable, too. Christina wasn't trying to be Charlotte Church, the young classical sensation. This was about having fun, enjoying herself, doing what she did best.

The days in the studios were long, or at least as long as she was allowed to make them under the California juvenile labor laws. There was tutoring in the morning, and from there it was off to work. In the studio, where everything was in artificial light, so it was impossible to tell day from night, there would be take after take of a song, trying different things, listening to playbacks, and seeing what worked and what didn't. There would be breaks, so she didn't end up straining her voice—any voice is actually a pretty delicate instrument—and then back to work on the track some more. While going in and singing to a backing track sounds easy, there's a lot involved. Even when the lead vocal has been nailed, there are still the backing vocals to be done—and Christina did a lot of those herself, too, all overdubbed several times. It was a process that couldn't be rushed, not if everything was going to be perfect. It was like assembling a jigsaw puzzle; every piece had its place, and they all needed to fit exactly.

For Christina, every day was a new experience, and an exhausting one at that. She'd go to her new home at night (and the people she was staying with made sure she was well looked after) more or less ready to collapse. Being a singer might have sounded glamorous, but the actual procedure of making a record was simply draining. She didn't have the energy to be out and about, attending the right parties or being seen at the right restaurants. This was about work, and being as professional as she could be. Her voice had to be in the best possible shape, and that meant getting plenty of sleep, and staying very aware of her health.

Professionalism was the key word. Christina had been working toward this for almost ten years. Now that her big opportunity had arrived, she wasn't about to blow it by trying to live the high life. She was totally focused on making this record the very best it could be. So few people had a chance like this, and she knew she was starting something that would last a lifetime. That made it very easy to resist the outside temptations. Music had been the center of her life for so long that now that she was really doing it, everything seemed perfect. She didn't want any more than that.

It was hard work, but it was magical, too. To hear all the hours she and everyone else had put in to a song come together was amazing. In the studio, she was able to hear herself with a special clarity. The producers gave her direction, and she was more than happy to listen. She'd been singing for a long time, but she was still young, and not always sure of herself, even if she seemed on the surface to exude confidence.

In the past, she'd always been surprised when she read that a record could take months, or even a year or more to make, but now she was beginning to understand how that could happen. You couldn't push too hard, or it all became sloppy. So she continued to plunge herself in to the work every day, surfacing only on the weekend, when she could do things like take trips to Disneyland or wander around the tourist sites of Hollywood to recharge her batteries.

It was nine years since she'd been to Los Angeles, and while she remembered her first trip very well, it was almost as if it had happened to a different person. She was grown up now, an adult in everything but legal terms. There were times she still felt very young, but that was natural. She missed her family, and, to her surprise, there were times when she missed Wexford, where everything seemed on a much more human scale than Los Angeles. At least the freeways weren't always jammed there, and the waitresses didn't always have an attitude.

Still, there was a sense of liberation in being away from home, even if she was staying in someone else's home. It really did emphasize to her that she was an adult, that this was going to be her career, and that, even though she was being tutored, she wouldn't have to return to school when it was all over. A certain phase of her life had ended, and she'd started the second chapter already.

It was exciting, there was no doubt about it. She could be exactly who she wanted to be, and she didn't have to conform to any school rules. But that didn't mean she was about to rush out and get covered with tattoos or piercings. Not her style at all. She was very much the normal girl. She liked fashion, cool hair, cool shoes, and getting her nails done, but she wasn't about to make any changes to her body. How could she go back home and face Shelly if she'd done something like that?

With each note she sang, each tutoring session, and each trip on the L.A. roads, she felt as if she were discovering more about herself. At home, everything had been laid out and she knew what to expect. And while her days were fully accounted for out here, it was different, as if it had more to do with *her*. She was in a constant state of excitement; every new thing amazed her. The several times a week when she called her mother, she was so full of news and ideas that she just gushed. There was so much to tell—the way a track was coming together, who she'd seen in a restaurant or on the street, what the weather was like, some item of clothing she'd bought.

Most of all, she just loved to sing, and she was getting plenty of opportunity to do that. Every day she was exercising her voice. Even on the weekends and during her time off, she would sing alone. It had become as natural to her as breathing by now.

Every one of the songs for the album offered its own challenges, whether in delivery, range or emotion. She reveled in it, being able to immerse herself in the tunes, to help bring them alive with her voice. This creation was a kind of satisfaction she'd never known before.

Soon, she knew, this part would be over, and she'd probably be glad of it after spending a good six months out in Los Angeles, living most of the time in studios. But she'd learned a lot of restraint over the course of that time.

"I wanted to start belting with the first verse, and [Ron Fair] did teach me how to not let the cat out of the bag too soon, how to keep it soft at first."

That was an important lesson; you didn't have to show it all at once. You could let things build gradually, and increase the intensity. Still, no one had expected Christina to be fully formed as she entered the sessions. Her voice was remarkable, but at her age she couldn't know everything yet. And there would be a lot of material that worked best toward her bluesier range, while still sounding contemporary. Like Mariah, she was the kind of singer who could transcend generations, and appeal as much to the baby boomers as their children. Someone like that was very rare, and needed to be nurtured—which was exactly what Fair was doing.

Chapter Seven

Eventually, of course, all the recording was completed to everyone's satisfaction. The tracks still had to be mixed, but that wouldn't involve Christina. There were still some things left for her to do on the coast: have a makeover and shoot pictures for publicity and the CD cover.

She had the eyes, big and soulful and blue, and she had the face, but there was still the hair. She needed a style that was original and striking, but not too weird. After plenty of consultations, there was an idea, which over the course of a few hours in a salon became reality. Very blond, framing her face, coming down at the back just beyond her neck. It was perfect. Impossible not to notice, it was exactly the kind of do that could be copied by girls everywhere—much like the famous style of Jennifer Aniston from *Friends*.

That was hardly the extent of it, though. There was the makeup, working on her eyebrows, using cosmetics to highlight her eyes and make them look even bigger and deeper, accentuating her high cheekbones, and filling out her lips, until everything looked just right.

Finally, they chose her clothes. Christina wasn't especially tall, but she could be dressed to make her seem taller. She had a long midriff, so crop tops and hip-hugging pants and skirts became the order of the day, to accent that long leanness. White set off her delicate coloring especially well.

When the total effect had been achieved, it was time for the photographs. The sessions ran over a couple of days, and were far more exhausting for Christina than any singing. When she was in a studio it was all about her voice, and what she could do. This was about the way she looked and came across, whether on location outside, or in some photo studio. Rolls and rolls of film were shot. She was dressed in many different outfits, some white, some dark. Between rolls, assistants would refresh her makeup, make minute adjustments, change the lighting. She had to pose for hours, and still look natural.

It wasn't easy for her to enter the new world of glamour she was going to have to inhabit. She loved the clothes—what girl wouldn't want to have her choice of designer labels laid out in front of her?—but the posing was wearying. Her nails were long and exotic: done in two colors, everything made her look like a model, but it was going to take a long time before this all really felt like *her*. When she looked in the mirror, the person she saw wasn't the girl who'd just turned eighteen, who was about to head home for Christmas. This was . . . well, she wasn't sure, but she understood she'd have to get used to this new image.

She knew that was part of the game, that a record was going to put her in the public eye, and that this was the way it would have to be from now on. There'd be private moments—until the record came out, quite a few of them—but in public she had to keep this up. No jeans and old sweatshirts any more, but the kind of clothes and look guaranteed to turn heads. It came with the territory. And she knew she wanted the territory, so she was willing to pay the price.

A little before Christmas, she packed her bags, said goodbye to everyone in Los Angeles, and boarded a Pittsburgh-bound flight at LAX. It was time to go home. On the way out, she'd brought the things she needed. Now, returning, her bags bulged, there were other bags checked, and she was dressed in her best clothes. The new Christina was going to surprise her family.

They were all waiting for her at the airport. She recognized them, but it took a few seconds before they saw her. She looked so . . . glamorous, so much older. The person who'd gone away had been a daughter, a sister, a granddaughter. The woman in heels and a designer dress was a sophisticated young woman. She'd grown while she was away. Not so much physically, although her appearance was radically different. She gave off more confidence, a real sense of adulthood. But once she was hugging everyone, she was exactly the same Christina she'd always been, crying with joy to be back with the people she loved, even if it meant the mascara was running down her cheeks.

It was a wonderful reunion. Being away had been fun, and her time had been full, but it was great to be home again. One thing Christina did notice, as they drove from the airport out to Wexford, was that everything seemed so much smaller than she remembered it. The houses, the stores, even the malls seemed not as large as life, and they passed through the city and the suburbs more quickly than she'd expected.

Christmas itself was perfect. She'd been able to buy presents for everyone in Los Angeles, the kind of things they'd never find locally. There was even something special for her half brother Michael, who'd just turned three. The family spent the entire day together, giving gifts, eating, watching television, and just enjoying each other's company. It was stress-free and wonderful, exactly the kind of break Christina needed after the last few months.

Once Christmas was over, Christina had friends to see, and gossip to catch up on. Of course, her friends couldn't believe the way she looked now, or the kind of clothes she was wearing. It was as if she'd already become a star. But she wasn't; she was still the same Christina.

The new year meant a return to being tutored when the others went back to school. For the moment, there was little else on her plate except to learn. It would be several months before her record came out, and as 1998 turned into 1999, her calendar was pretty free. Even the publicity machine wouldn't really gear up for a few months, although press releases about her were already being distributed. For now she could pretty much kick back for a few months, relax, and focus on getting her high school diploma.

The start of the year did bring one major thrill, when her friend Britney Spears enjoyed major pop success. With not only a single but also an album topping the charts, Britney had beaten Christina to the punch, but that didn't matter.

"When Britney's album came out, I was the first to buy it," she says, and why would she lie? They'd been close friends on *The New Mickey Mouse Club*, and they'd kept in touch, even if there hadn't really been any opportunities for them to meet since. Christina was ecstatic when Britney went to Number One. It showed that the girls could do it just as well as the boys—which was important. If she did as well, she'd be over the moon.

In fact, they did get a chance to meet, at an awards show in February. Somehow or other, people had planted rumors of jealousy between Christina and Britney. The rumors were ridiculous, and completely untrue, and the way they behaved—spending the evening together, talking and laughing—showed just how false the "rift" was. They had a lot of catching up to do, a lot of notes to compare. They'd both grown a lot since the last time they'd met, and they'd both seen their careers come a long way. Britney was a star, and Christina, whose album still wouldn't be released for quite a while, was the wannabe (which was probably how the evil rumors had begun). But the bottom line was that they were friends.

The awards show was her introduction to another side of show business—schmoozing, the party atmosphere. But again, it was part of the game. She was expected to attend these things now, although she would rather have been singing in a club somewhere, getting a chance to exercise her voice properly.

It was a frustrating time for her. The record was done, the mixing complete. She had a copy of it at home, which she played often, and which had amazed her family. She'd seen the cover art and the pictures they were going to use for promotion. If it was all ready, why were they waiting to release it, she wondered. Instead of being at promotional parties, or at home, she could have been touring and singing. But those business decisions weren't hers to make; she understood that. The label had invested a lot of time and money in her. They knew what they were doing.

She knew the record sounded good, that everyone had worked very hard on it. But she also knew it wasn't completely representative of the way she really was. "If music becomes too pop, I lose interest," she explains. "I need to be challenged." But at eighteen, pop music, and the people who buy it, were her market. And if the material really had challenged her, would it be likely to sell? In other words, there had to be a real balance between the artistic and commercial considerations.

The label had already decided to kick things off in the summer by releasing "Genie in a Bottle" as a single. Surprisingly enough, Christina wasn't too happy with the idea. To her, it was the album's most obvious track. It didn't really demand anything of her as a singer, and certainly gave no real indication of her abilities. But the matter wasn't really up for discussion. The fact was that the label believed it could be a major hit, and that was what they were after. And, Christina had to admit, it was what she wanted too. A hit single would establish her in a very big way. She wanted people to recognize her, to asked for her autograph.

"I know a lot of people would hate that," she admits. "But not me. I've been waiting all my life for this moment."

Just how much she'd been waiting for it had come home to her when she was in New York for that awards show. She was in Times Square, browsing through the racks in a large record store, when she'd glanced up, looked . . . and then looked again. On the other side of the store was Fred Durst of Limp Bizkit. At first she thought it couldn't be him—he was a star, what was he doing here?—but it was. She began to move toward him, determined to get his autograph. But by the time she reached where he'd been, he was nowhere in sight, just vanished. She was downhearted, but it did make her think. She wanted to be him, to have people coming up and asking for *her* autograph. After all, wasn't that why

she'd done all this? It was why she was putting a CD
out, to be heard, to get acceptance. And the way the
market worked, the only way that would happen was if
she had a hit.

It certainly wasn't that she was ashamed of anything
on the record—far from it. But she wanted people to
realize that there was a lot more to her than just pop
music. After all, this was the girl who'd started out by
singing everything from *The Sound of Music*. But it was
cool. If they believed that strongly in "Genie in a Bottle," she was more than happy to go along with it, and
do everything she could to make it into a smash. It was
the very least she could do to repay the label for the
faith they'd shown in her. The fact was, the song stood
an excellent chance of being a hit, and the market was
now very open to young artists—a complete reversal
from the way it had been just three years before. And
Britney had opened the way for young female solo artists.

The other notable development of 1999 didn't pass
Christina by either, as Ricky Martin became a sensation
and Jennifer Lopez scored a massive hit: the huge surge
of interest in Latin music. This was something that was
in Christina's blood, a part of her biology and heritage
that she'd gotten from her father. Since her father had
been born in Ecuador and her mother had been a Spanish
interpreter, Spanish had been the second language
around the house when she was small. She genuinely
liked Latin music, so if she were to do a Latin album
some day, it would be a natural move. Most people who
saw her name naturally assumed she was Latin anyway,
at least until they saw the blond hair and blue eyes.

But that was another plan for the future, something
to be filed and savored. For now she could retreat to her

bedroom in the basement of the house in Wexford, her hideaway. No matter where she went, this would always be the place that felt like home, with her stuffed animals, posters, prints, and the lava lamp plugged in by the bed, sending reflections across the ceiling. Here she could sing just for herself, as she did when there was no one else to listen. She could pick up her hairbrush and use it as a microphone. She realized she'd come a long way from the days when that was her only outlet. Now it was going to be real. After a tutoring session now she could come down to her room, look at her CD, and know it was going to happen.

"If I was in school now," she reflects, "I'd be looking out of the window, thinking, 'What if I'd gone out there to pursue my dream?' "

But, with her mother's blessing, that was exactly what she had done.

Very soon the publicity machine would move into action, and she'd be giving interviews, be doing all kinds of things to be more visible before the first single came out. She'd be on the road a lot. It was going to be hectic, but it would be fun.

Before any of that, however, something very important had to be done—there was the video to be shot for "Genie in a Bottle." The storyboard had already been completed, and director Diane Martel, who'd worked with stars like Mariah Carey, was set to work on it. It was going to be shot on location—on the beach in Malibu, California, so Christina was going to have to get back on a plane and head west again.

There were rehearsals, of course. The dance routines were choreographed, and Christina learned them quickly, much to the admiration of Jermaine Brown, who'd put it all together. And there would be costumes, most particularly Christina's genie halter top, made of beads.

It would be a night shoot, which, in theory, shouldn't have been that big a deal. This was Southern California, where it never got cold. But that night it *did* get cold.

"I was freezing," Christina remembers. "But once the music came on, my body just warmed up."

Of course, there were blankets she could huddle under between shots—and she did. But there was also a constant stream of hair and makeup people fussing over her, making sure she looked absolutely perfect for each new shot.

And, of course, there was a large cast of extras—mostly teens, involved as dancers. But there was one guy who had a special role—that of Christina's love interest in the video. His name was Ryan McTavish. He'd been personally selected by the star, because "he was swarthy with a baby face."

One thing no one could have predicted was that there'd be a party going on in the house next door to where they were shooting. Not just any party, either. The house belonged to the mother of Dean Cain, the actor who'd played Superman on television. It was her birthday, and her famous son was in attendance. In fact, he even stopped by the shoot, which left Christina "so psyched."

The shoot began once darkness had fallen, and was set to carry on until it was done (or dawn arrived, whichever happened first). By rights, Christina should have been exhausted, but there was not only the excitement of making the video, there was also the fact that Christina was a night person, one who regularly stayed up late.

To her, all of this fuss was odd. Like any teen, she

watched MTV, and she understood that videos required a lot of effort, time, and money. Exactly how much, though, hadn't been apparent until that night. What seemed effortless on the screen involved dozens of people working their butts off for hours. By the time it was done, she'd heard her song so many times it was almost surprising she wasn't sick of it.

There were takes and retakes on the dancing, as it was shot from different angles. Lights had to be adjusted for each new shot. But Christina was just as committed as anyone to making it the best possible video—probably even more so, because it was her song and she was the star. A great deal hinged on this doing well. If the single sank, and the album didn't do well, her career might as well be over. Second chances didn't come along too often in the music business, particularly in the disposable medium known as pop music. You sank or you swam, and Christina wanted a long career, so she needed to swim—and swim powerfully.

Finally, in the wee small hours, everything was finished, and Christina huddled with Diane Martel to watch a playback of the completed video—a very rough cut which would be smoothed out in the editing room.

"It's weird," Christina says of watching herself. "I liked it though."

And, as anyone who's seen the clip on television knows, what's not to like? Christina looks great, showing what must be a tremendously long, supple midriff. There's a story, there's dancing. Everything looks and sounds so good. And, in spite of the cold during filming, it all seems as if it were taking place on some balmy summer night, somewhere magical and special. But that is the spell of music and film.

With the video completed, everything was in place,

all the pieces ready and waiting for the release of the single.

By now, Christina had completed her home study course, and had earned her high school diploma, something she thought of as a genuine, tangible achievement. After some miserable times at school, to be able to finish on her own was something of a relief. And she knew full well that she'd never have been able to juggle school and her musical commitments her last year. Something would have been forced to give, and it would probably have been school. But now it was over, and done. She wouldn't have a real graduation, and tutoring didn't exactly allow for a prom, but those were minor things, really. She was now free, adult, and ready to take on the world!

Publicity would be the next step, and that was going to present a slight problem. By living in Wexford, Christina was somewhat out of the loop, away from the center of things in New York and Los Angeles, as her manager explained to her. She needed to be available and accessible, especially now. The best thing she could do would be to move to one of those cities. That was something pretty major to consider. She was just eighteen, she'd never lived on her own before, and really hadn't been considering it now. She wasn't sure she was ready for it yet. But if it was necessary, then that was what she had to do.

Los Angeles was definitely out of the question. It was just too far away from home; there were too many hours separating her from her family. New York intimidated her, but at least it wasn't too far away. She could always drive home—at least she'd be able to if she ever got her driver's license. So it looked as if New York was the answer, but finding an apartment there wasn't the simplest task in the world.

Having connections at a record company did help, though, and before long, Christina had come up with a place on the trendy Upper West Side, somewhere secure and homey, which she furnished somewhat sparsely; it wasn't as if she'd be spending a whole lot of time there in the next year, what with publicity, then touring, as well as rest breaks in Pennsylvania. It just had to be functional, that was all she needed for now. Settling in, it seemed strange to be completely alone, and not always comfortable. All her life she'd been used to having people around her, and she missed them.

Her days, though, were suddenly fully booked. There were photo shoots, and interviews, as the label prepared to release "Genie in a Bottle." They wanted the world to know about Christina, and to see that there were big differences between her and every other teenager releasing albums. For now, though, it was inevitable she'd be compared to Britney and others, and that scared her. And so did the idea of her being a disposable commodity, a fad who faded quickly; that was something she definitely didn't want.

Already some people were talking about a rivalry between Christina and Britney that had never existed, and that understandably upset her. The two were still close friends, and very supportive of each other. They were simply two singers in the same business, that was all. But it was true that, by virtue of her big voice, Christina came across as more adult. And she wanted to be able to take chances, which was one reason she'd been booked on some dates for the Lilith Fair, the all-female tour organized by Sarah McLachlan, that had spent the last few summers going around North America. *That* would be a major challenge to her as an artist. The bills generally comprised women from the more alternative or folkie ends of the musical spectrum. Christina knew she was going to be perceived as a pure pop artist, and that acceptance was going to be an uphill battle. But that was what she relished. She'd already decided that for those dates she wouldn't be the pop diva. Instead, she'd be accompanied only by a pianist, and sing material she loved, covers of Etta James and others.

Of course, that would only be one outlet. She'd get to exercise her pop muscles in other dates that were currently being assembled. But the Lilith Fair, she thought, might end up being the most satisfying, if only because it would offer her a chance to really be herself.

The weeks sped by until May, and the release to radio and television of "Genie in a Bottle" (it wouldn't be in the stores until June 22). It would rank among the most memorable days in her life, waking up, switching on the radio and hearing herself, then flipping channels on the television and seeing her video on MTV. This was still the type of thing that happened to other people, not to Christina Aguilera of Wexford, PA. And she had to admit that "Genie" sounded *right* on the radio. It was catchy, the beats were cool, and it truly did have all the ingredients of a hit. Even if it didn't show what she could do, it had something.

With the record out, she actually had a little time on her hands, and got to thinking about some of the real-life things she was missing—like a senior prom. She kept telling herself it didn't matter, that people would treat her strangely anyway, but finally she decided she *should* go, even if she was really no longer a student at the school. She called up her best friend Marcy and told her, "Let's have a little fun with this. Set me up with a really cute blind date."

Marcy did just that. But a male friend of Christina's had been hoping to escort her, and was a little hurt that she wouldn't be going with him. So Christina ended up with two dates, and in the end that was probably just as well, because very few of the girls were willing to talk to her—nor would they let their dates dance with her. It wasn't exactly the romantic event she'd hoped it would be, and not one to fold into her book of great memories. But that was fine. It let her know that it was the others who had a problem, not her.

"All I want to do is be normal," she says. "But really it's other people who won't let me be that way."

To be fair, not many people attend their senior prom when their record is all over the radio and TV, but Christina had wanted to show she was just like them, to extend the hand of friendship, which very few seemed willing to take. It was a shame. But it made her all the more determined to focus on her career. And given the way her calendar looked for the next few months, that promised to be quite easy. She wasn't going to have a minute to think about much else.

Chapter Eight

In some ways it was as much about the look as the voice, and Christina wasn't too happy about that. She liked to dress up, she loved her new do, but she wanted to be accepted for what she could do, not what she wore or how she presented herself. But for television, that was important.

Her look was definitely one of the sparks of the video, but more than anything, it would be radio that helped kick the song along. By the time it was released, there was already a huge demand for it. People heard it and loved it, and wanted to buy it, which was exactly what they went out and did. In its first week, it entered the charts, and simply kept climbing. The video was in the top ten on MTV's *Total Request Live* every time the show was on the air. It all seemed completely unreal to Christina.

She had to fly out to Los Angeles for a photo shoot for *Mademoiselle*, which, purely on the strength of the single, and her age, was naming her one of the people to watch in the new millennium. There she had her first brush with the kind of public recognition she'd dreamed about. She was stocking up on MAC cosmetics at the Beverly Center, when "Suddenly, these girls come up and they're screaming 'Are you Christina Aguilera? "Genie in a Bottle"?' They had just bought my single and had it with them. Then they went out and bought a disposable camera to take my picture." Recognition! Maybe it didn't make her a star, but it meant that someone knew who she was besides her family and a few people in the record industry.

Actually, it was quite a few more than that. Her single was in the top ten, and selling *very* strongly. The next week it stood at number two, and then, the week after, it had climbed that final place, all the way to the top of the singles chart.

Now that was entering the world with a real bang! Her very first release, all the way to Number One! Outside of fairy tales, that just didn't happen. When Christina was called by the label, to tell her the news, she couldn't believe it. Being at number two had been beyond her wildest dreams, but this? It was totally unreal. Until she saw it in black and white, and even more calls began to come in for television appearances, she couldn't be certain it was true, that it wasn't some weird misprint, or someone just trying to mess with her head.

It wasn't just the chart position that was overwhelming, it was the sheer number of records she was selling. The single had already sold over half a million copies, qualifying it for a gold record, and it was far from its peak. "Genie in a Bottle" was the song of the summer. Everywhere you went, it was playing, in clubs, gyms, on TV, radio—you simply couldn't get away from it. So Christina had to admit the record company had definitely been right in their choice of single, even if she felt it didn't do her voice justice. And now she was in demand, and every day was turning into a very full day. MTV wanted to interview her. Radio stations wanted to talk to her. And there was still a full month before her album would appear. It was madness of a kind she'd never imagined—but she was loving every second of it, even while she wondered how long it could last.

The answer was that it could last quite a long time. The next week's charts appeared, and she was *still* Number One, and that thrilled her just as much as reaching the top spot. There was already talk of a fall tour, maybe teaming Christina up for dates with TLC or 'N Sync, which really would be a dream come true, since two of them were old friends.

But even as her single disappeared out of stores by the truckload, some people were dissing the lyrics, saying it was full of sexual connotations. Christina was quick to deny that allegation, pointing out that it was really about respect and empowerment. When women spoke up and demanded to be treated in the same way as men, Christina argued, it was taken wrongly—and the same with appearances, too.

She was right, of course—people were always far too eager to read too much into a word or a gesture—but in the long run, it probably wouldn't alter things, although she was determined to try. That was one of her goals, to be able to speak her mind, to hopefully break down a few doors for young female singers, who were all too often treated as just disposable product. And the more success and visibility she enjoyed, the more people would be likely to listen to her. For now, both success and visibility didn't seem to be a problem for her, as the single stayed at Number One for a third and then a fourth week, doing way better than anyone—particularly Christina—could have dreamed. By now, it wasn't a case of publicists getting her on shows—the shows were coming to her, wanting her to be a guest, just in time for her album release. There'd be *Total Request Live*, *The Tonight Show with Jay Leno*, and *MTV's House of*

Style as well as some live appearances all within a few days of each other at the end of August. Most surprising, but most gratifying of all, *Beverly Hills 90210* had her slated to sing in an episode to be aired in September.

"Genie in a Bottle" stayed at the top of the *Billboard* singles chart for a total of five weeks—an incredible run for a debut. It was far more than anyone could have expected, or even hoped for. But it was reaching the point where the label had to divert attention from just one song to a whole album full of them.

Prior to all that, however, Christina was spending a lot of her time on the road. Late July saw her somewhere she hadn't been for a few years—Japan. This time she wasn't just the sidekick to a Japanese pop star, but a star in her own right, promoting "Genie in a Bottle" and her upcoming album. She arrived back in New York on August 1, and immediately had to begin rehearsing for her three Lilith Fair dates, which would be on August 10, 11, and 12, in Columbus, Cincinnati, and—this would be a major event—in her hometown of Pittsburgh, as close to Wexford as the tour was going to get.

"I am not going to be singing 'Genie in a Bottle,' " she explained on MTV. "It's a time where I think I can get in front of a bunch of women and really sing my heart out to just piano and vocal. It's just a piano and a mike, and that's it. I'll get bluesy with Etta James's 'At Last,' which is one of my favorite songs."

It was a daring, and very unlikely move, perhaps the equivalent of, say, the Backstreet Boys turning up at Woodstock and singing '50s doo-wop. Christina's fame was as a pop star, someone not to be taken too seriously, in other words. But she wanted to prove that, although she was young, there was a lot of depth to her, and that she was in music not solely for fame, but for the love of the music itself. That, after all, was what had started her on the path, and would keep her going on it for a long time to come.

And being accompanied solely by a pianist meant she would essentially be naked on stage, relying on her voice to carry her through. No fancy arrangements, no beats, just her, the focus completely on her. It would be a kind of release, the chance to do something completely different after focusing on her album, and before she was plunged back into a series of shows to promote the record. She also loved being on the stage, and the chance to surprise people was too good to refuse. It hadn't been easy, convincing people that she'd be a good addition to the Lilith dates, but she was determined to go out there and knock them dead, to make people understand there was a lot more to her than they'd seen in her video.

Playing Pittsburgh, in particular, meant a great deal to her. She knew there'd be people there she'd gone to school with, people all too ready to write her off and bad-mouth her. More than anything, she wanted to show them, make them eat their words. Maybe, in the overall scheme of things, it didn't really matter, but it would give her a great deal of satisfaction to go back, both as a star and as a performer.

After that, and a short break, it was back on the publicity merry-go-round. Then she headed out to California again, to appear on *The Tonight Show with Jay Leno*. She was also set to appear at an event dubbed Teenapalooza, with Joey McIntyre, at the Greek Theater in Los Angeles. Sponsored by the UPN Network, it would be Christina's first chance to really sing songs from her album, and to appear as a teen idol. The event would be taped, and would air on the 31st of August as part of UPN's *Summer Music Mania '99*.

The biggest event of all, however, was the release of her album, titled simply *Christina Aguilera*. After all this time, it was finally going to appear. To her, it seemed like something she'd worked on a long time ago, almost as if a different person had done it. But when she heard the tracks, it all came back to her, completely fresh. This was what it had all been about. There was still a huge thrill in holding it, in seeing her name on the cover, in knowing that she'd done this.

She understood that having a big single didn't automatically translate into major sales for the album. Singles and albums were two different species. So she was completely flabbergasted when, on the week of its release, her album jumped straight into the chart at Number One! It was something she hadn't expected, particularly because it was going head to head with the new Puff Daddy album which, logic dictated, should have easily outsold hers. But there it was, in black and white in *Billboard*. Christina Aguilera owned the top album in America. At that point you could probably have knocked her over with a feather. Since June the shocks had been coming one on top of another, but this was undoubtedly the biggest one of all. People liked what she did enough to go out and spend fifteen dollars on her record—and not just a few of them either.

Christina Aguilera would only hold the top spot for one week, but that didn't matter. She'd done something very few people manage, especially on a debut. Top single and top album. Britney had managed it, of course, but the women who did were very rare indeed. It made Christina a success right from the word go. But her album certainly didn't vanish; it was sticking around in the top ten, and still selling thousands of copies a week—in fact, five weeks after its release, it had sold more than *two million* copies, an absolutely staggering number. That was faster than any of the boy bands had managed with their first albums, and fully established Christina as a teen diva—although she didn't really care for that term. She was a teenager, it was true, and she had a big voice. But *diva* didn't sound right, and she didn't want any allowances made for her age. She was a singer, and wanted to be compared to the best.

Though it was selling like the proverbial hotcakes, the reviews were not flattering. *People* criticized the "watery R&B arrangements," and summed it up as "talented young singer adrift in sap." (At least they considered her talented: she was described as having "potent pipes.") *Entertainment Weekly* was equally unimpressed, calling the record "frustratingly erratic," inasmuch as half of it seemed designed to appeal to teens, and half to their parents. Still, writer Beth Johnson did note that Christina was "preternaturally piped," which was undeniable to anyone who heard the record.

There was a real gap, then, between those who were paid to listen to music, and those who spent their own money on it, and the bottom line was that those who were shelling out their hard-earned dollars for *Christina Aguilera* couldn't be wrong; they were voting with their wallets. And that, let's face it, was more powerful than any words. The video for "Genie in a Bottle" remained a constant feature on MTV's *Total Request Live*, radio couldn't get enough of her music . . . she was simply everywhere.

There was even talk of her remaking one of the album's ballads, "I Turn to You," in Spanish, the first real acknowledgment of both her Latin roots and the fact that a large portion of the population in America uses Spanish as their primary or secondary language.

*   *   *

There was nothing fancy about the cover of *Christina Aguilera*. Just a stunning close-up photo of the girl herself, showing the shape of her face, and how large her eyes are. There was her name, printed in black and white, and some sort of symbol—possibly a ring—next to it. The back cover was also sparse: Another picture of Christina in a crop top, showing plenty of midriff, the song titles, and the address of her fan club. Yes, she did already have one, and in the wake of her hit single, the websites from fans had begun blooming like flowers.

The leadoff track was *that* song, the one that had captivated the nation for the summer, "Genie in a Bottle," just to make sure the record started off in the strongest possible way. It was a slinky piece, with cool, interesting beats propelling the melody. The song was written by Steve Kipner, David Frank, and Pam Sheyne, and produced by Frank and Kipner, both former members of the System. Sheyne had done the vocal arrangement, which seemed simple, but which was actually quite complex, with Christina herself doing the additional vocal arrangement. It was a complex song on every level, in fact: vocally, instrumentally, rhythmically, and lyrically. A lot of people thought it was simply about sex, but if you looked more closely, it was actually about love and respect, two very important things. It was easy to see why it had become so popular. It stood out from the crowd of mass-produced songs—it was clever, inventive, and had a supremely catchy chorus.

From there it was straight into R&B, which gave Christina a much better chance to exercise her vocal chops. "What a Girl Wants" was written by Shelly Peiken and Guy Roche, with Roche producing. He had plenty of experience in the R&B field; he'd worked with

Brandy, Dru Hill, Aaliya, and K-Ci and JoJo, and he utilized all his experience on this jam, with Christina and Shelly Peiken working together on the background vocals. Christina's bluesy tone got a real chance to shine on the song, showing she could not only get deep and throaty, but also catch all the high notes she needed too. This was really what she did well, and a real indication of how mature her voice was; anyone who didn't know Christina's story would listen to the song and think the singer was much older than eighteen. It was impossible to fault her performance, confident and assured, floating over the chorus and letting her voice play so well—in other words, all the hallmarks of someone who knew exactly what her voice could do, and who'd worked hard on it for years. This exactly described Christina, who had made herself into a true professional. And it was also the sound of someone who was going to be around for a long time to come.

Diane Warren was a veteran songwriter, with many, many hits to her credit over the years, for a wide variety of artists. "I Turn to You" was one of her contributions to Christina's album, which she executive-produced— she'd certainly reached the stage of deserving that status. The track was produced by Guy Roche. It started with the sound of thunder, before keyboard chords wafted in and Christina's voice entered. As one review noted, the song was not dissimilar to Celine Dion's "Because You Loved Me"—which Warren had also written. But it did showcase the control Christina had over her voice: the way she could let a note float, the restraint she'd learned during recording, her ability to let a song build, to mesmerize with her vocals, and the fact that she could have a remarkable range when she wanted or needed to use it, moving effortlessly between octaves. It announced to everyone that Christina was very much the real deal, in the same class as Mariah or Whitney, and with Christina providing some of the background vocals, too, she had it all sewn up. Between the first three tracks, she'd pretty much covered the spectrum of possibilities for the album. While it probably wasn't as adventurous as she'd have liked, it gave a very fair—and glowing—picture of Christina's abilities. She was, beyond any shadow of a doubt, a shining star.

"So Emotional," like "Genie," was pop music with a dance beat. Penned by Franne Golde and Tom Snow and produced by Ron Harris (who was also responsible for the keyboards and drum programming), it was the type of song that had *future hit* written all over it. There was a bounce to it, and the title was repeated often enough to be hammered home in the listener's mind. And it had a definite R&B feel, with Christina's voice fully front and center, able to get a good workout. It was, in essence, a very simple song, but arranged cleverly enough, with a strong bridge that took it in a slightly different, more balladic direction, before returning to the direct groove. And there was a great deal of subtlety not only in Christina's vocal work, but in her leads, which were overdubbed, and her layers of backing vocals. The arrangement played to her real strengths—the many ways she could use her voice and the way she could make even the smallest phrase count. It was a trait that was beyond most young singers, who hadn't yet developed the authority to make something like that work for them. But that was Christina. Not only did she sound older than her years, but her vocal mannerisms were also far more mature, too. She didn't need to hit you over the head with the power of her voice; she had many more weapons in her vocal arsenal, and could use them all equally well.

There was plenty more pure pop, in the form of "Come on Over (All I Want Is You)," the same type of Scandinavian pop music that had helped both BSB and 'N Sync. Written by Paul Rein and Johan Aberg, and produced by them, along with Aaron Zigman, it was a confection, but still utterly irresistible. In many ways, the basic song structure dated back to the '50s, but the touches applied to it were pure '90s, with lots of studio wizardry, and layered Christinas on vocals and backing vocals. The real kicker, however, was the chorus, which just swept you up and carried you away. There was nothing fancy in the beats—there really didn't need to be on this, and less was definitely more in some regards. The song was strong enough to carry everything. No funk, just pop, and ideal as it stood, although it was unlikely to ever be anything more than an album track, since the style simply wasn't what the mass market in America seemed to want, though it worked perfectly within the context of an album. It was bubblegum, yes, but with great flavor and long-lasting taste. And who needed more than that in bubblegum, anyway? In some ways it was probably filler, but if all albums had filler that was this strong, records would be much improved. Perhaps the only thing it didn't do was cast a major spotlight on Christina's voice—all she could do was go along with the melody.

That was certainly not true of the next track, "Reflection," the song that had been the turning point for Christina. Aaron Zigman, who'd produced the previous song, was here too, this time as orchestral arranger. It was about as different from "Come on Over (All I Want Is You)" as it was possible to get on a single record. In many ways it was a classic Disney ballad, the type that seemed to turn up in almost every feature they released. It was very much Christina's "pure" (as opposed to bluesy) voice that was required here, and without that edge, she definitely sounded younger. She still applied a lot of control and restraint over the song, though, and easily touched that high E, the note that had gotten her to the point where she was today. Lyrically, it was very much a case of a teenage girl looking at herself and trying to figure out just who she was, which made it perfect for Christina at the time, a mirror of her own excitement and confusion. At the same time, there was no doubt it was very different from the rest of the album, even the ballads—a little more straightforward, and never trying to be more than clear. At the same time, though, its inclusion made sense. It connected Christina's past and present, and reminded people how she'd gotten her start, her big break. Plus, it was also the first most of her audience had ever heard of Christina, even if they didn't realize who she was at the time. Add to that the fact that it was a good song, and there was absolutely no reason for it not to be on the record.

Carl Sturken and Evan Rogers, who'd worked with people like 'N Sync, Boyzone, and the Brand New Heavies, upped the tempo a bit with "Love for All Seasons," which they wrote and produced. They only upped it a little bit, though. While not quite a slow jam, this was the kind of song that was made for dancing close to someone you really cared about. With a feel that successfully mixed pop and R&B, it had a very easy grace, although it offered quite a challenge to a singer, in terms of fitting the vocal lines around the melody, and also in the slides up and down the octaves it required. But Christina relished a challenge, or even two, and she coped with them easily. One thing it did show, though, was something a few people had commented on—the fact that her singing style wasn't unlike Mariah Carey's. To Christina, who'd idolized Mariah since she was eleven, that was a high compliment indeed. It was easy to believe that Mariah would have tackled the song in exactly the same manner. Of course, Mariah hadn't been that old when she hit with her debut, either—the parallels between the two as vocalists were there, and offered an indication that Christina might well be able to emulate her heroine in terms of success.

Diane Warren was best known for her ballads, but "Somebody's Somebody" wasn't in that tradition, moving the bpms (beats per minute) up just a tad, to something shy of mid-tempo. Again, she was not only the composer, but also the executive producer, with Khris Kellow behind the board for the song (as well as contributing keyboards and programming). Even Ron Fair, the A&R man who'd brought Christina to RCA, took a hand, playing some keyboards. It was a delicious song, with strong lyrical wordplay, the kind that occurred all too rarely in the '90s, and the R&B groove that was suggested by the arrangement fit Christina's voice like a glove. You could hear, as the verses climaxed, exactly how much she could give vocally if necessary, although she was holding herself back. And the web of background vocals that she spun was gorgeously sheer and magical, intertwining with her own lead. All in all, it offered a real indication that Christina could turn her hand to almost anything musically, although it would seem she'd been proving that all through the record; there wasn't a single weak performance from her. Nor did she feel the need to show off her abilities and range just for their own sake—everything she did was in service of putting the song across, not deliberately drawing attention to herself and her talent, which was both admirable and unusual, and marked her as a real team player.

That was evident, too, in "When You Put Your Hands on Me," written and produced by Robin Thicke and Pro J (J. Gass), who also played much of the instrumentation on the track. It was a pop song, very carefully given a bit of an R&B makeover in its rhythms. The star of the show, however, was undoubtedly Christina, who layered her vocals beautifully, and who was able to give a very sexy inflection to her lines, which were, actually, not really about sex at all, but the feeling of meeting that special someone. But it was certainly true that few women of Christina's age could slither around a vocal line the way she could, or be anywhere near as subtle. All those years of singing in her room, of listening and learning, had fully paid off, giving her a maturity well beyond her tender years. Everything had built up to moments like this, where she knew instinctively what to do, and how to make it work perfectly. Not that she didn't get direction from the different producers she worked with. But the talent she'd been blessed with, her gift, had been developed for more than ten years. Early on in her life it had seemed as if she'd been born to sing—now it was obvious that was definitely the case. And with Mariah making strong moves towards hip-hop, there was a void for a good singer who could cover all the bases—a void Christina could happily, and easily, fill.

"Blessed" was a very straightforward, emotional song, an exquisite slow jam, cowritten and produced by Trevon Potts, who'd scored big before as the cowriter of Monica's "Angel of Mine." Its bluntness served it well as a love song, as smooth as a bird gliding through the air, but giving Christina a chance to sing her heart out, and inject plenty of feeling into the lyrics. She'd become a real master at involving herself in the song, a trait she'd had since the very beginning of her career, and one of the things that had helped her stand out from the pack. Like the previous tune, it brought to mind Mariah Carey's debut album, and there was nothing wrong with that. If *Christina Aguilera* could sell as strongly, and in as many countries, then an international superstar would be born—and if Christina could score as many Number One hits as Mariah, no one would be able to deny her stature. Of course, the market had changed since Mariah appeared on the scene in 1990, but that was no matter; Christina could deliver the goods in any style, and on any stage, as she'd already proved. So even though a song like "Blessed" didn't tax her too much, she was able to really put it across in a powerful fashion, the kind of piece that resonated with young, hopeful love. And that counted as much as anything else she'd ever recorded.

Things moved back to the dance floor for "Love Will Find a Way," another from the team of Carl Sturken and Evan Rogers, with Christina and Rogers providing the thick cushion of backing vocals, which offered as much of a hook as the chorus itself. Her ability to jump between octaves certainly added to the song's appeal, but at heart it was the beat that got people up and moving. Her voice was so good that it could propel the song, and when it cut to simply the overdubbed voices and a drumbeat, there was a special, genuine excitement about it, before the instruments kicked in and took it to an even higher level. The message, too, of love conquering all, was inspirational: bad times would always pass. Maybe

Christina didn't have someone in her life to whom she could sing the song directly, but it applied quite equally to her dreams, the aspirations that had kept her going for so long, and which still fired her—which was what she was really singing about. Dreams really could come true, and this record was a prime example of that. Whether it stood as a prime candidate for a second single had yet to be decided, but in some ways that didn't matter. It was a powerful album track, carefully placed to ease the excitement back up a notch, and serve as a reminder that Christina was a dance artist too—and a very good one at that.

Of course, like any album, *Christina Aguilera* had to end on a strong note, and in this case it was "Obvious," by Heather Holley, produced by Robert Hoffman. It was, perhaps, the most sophisticated song on the album, and the one that demanded the most from her. It was a love song, with a melody that was far from obvious. Putting it across properly demanded a great deal of artistry, particularly in the key changes. It was as close to a Broadway type of tune as the album came, and Christina delivered it superbly. On the bridge, she was able to let the bluesy side of her voice slide out briefly, before returning to the chorus and unleashing her power, then pulling back again. Its four minutes actually passed very quickly, like a spell, and it made an excellent finale to the record, the kind of piece that simply left you in awe of the voice you'd just experienced, and eager to hear it again to be certain you hadn't been mistaken. But there was no mistake. That was Christina, and those were the "pipes" that reviewers had praised, even if they weren't so keen on the material. Many would have ended a record on a faster note, but in this case, an out-and-out ballad made perfect sense, doing full justice to a remarkable voice. Twelve songs, a full variety of sound, and the kind of debut that would be the envy of any artist, new or established: "Genie in a Bottle" had promised, and *Christina Aguilera* delivered.

Chapter Nine

Christina couldn't have asked for a better introduction to her talent, and the reaction by people who were willing to send the album straight to Number One was a testament to what people thought about it. In August, *Teen People* had picked her as part of their New Talent roundup, and she'd certainly fulfilled that. But it was kind of a no-brainer, really; the record was utterly irresistible, the kind of thing that repaid repeated listenings, offering new depths every time, most particularly a track like "Obvious."

It was essentially a way to set the stage for what would be a long career, a record more adult than any teenager really had the right to be making, but which she carried off with great panache. Much as she loved Britney, there was absolutely no comparing the two of them. Christina's appeal was much wider-ranging, and, in a way, much more classic, less dependent on pop trends, which she could easily transcend. And *Christina Aguilera* certainly did show that. But it wasn't too surprising, since she herself looked to people like Mariah, Whitney, Madonna, and Janet Jackson, whom she called "the greats," people who kept developing, rather than standing still. And, as Christina says, "I hope with my career, I'll be able to do the same."

The photo shoots, the interviews, those were things that were expected of her. What she really wanted to do

was to sing, as often and for as long as she could. That
had been her focus for so long that she really didn't
know any other.

In truth, *Christina Aguilera* was nothing less than
spectacular. She'd exploded onto the scene, and among
people who watch MTV or listen to the radio, she'd
immediately become a household name. In a mere five
weeks, the record sold over two million copies, something almost unheard-of, and something which merely
confirmed how good people thought it was. Never mind
what the critics said—what did they know, anyway?
About the only thing they'd managed was to realize how
good her voice was.

"I've been waiting for this moment my whole life,"
she says, and she was certainly ready for it when it arrived, although she hadn't been expecting the overwhelming wave of support that did come.

The biography from her record company stated that
she might well be "the voice of her generation." Even
allowing for the standard amount of hype, it wasn't far
off the mark. She certainly had the ability, and being
less dependent on fad and fashion than many others, her
longevity seemed possible. Of course, it would take several years before any such title could be bestowed on
her, but she certainly had immediately established herself as a prime candidate.

There was never time to really sit back and bask in
her success, however. The more successful she became,
the more demands on her time, with everyone wanting
a piece of her—that was the name of the fame game.

To Christina's amazement and amusement, one thing
that had happened during the summer, as she became
more visible and more famous, was that movie offers
had come in. A few directors had approached her man-

ager about the possibility of her taking on roles in different films. It was flattering to be asked, and Christina had learned something about acting during her time on *The New Mickey Mouse Club*, but if something like that was ever going to happen, it certainly wouldn't be now. How could she even consider it when her world had to be music?

"Right now, I'm continuing to focus on my singing," she declares emphatically, and you'd better believe her. After working toward this for so many years, she's not about to let anything divert her from her goal, particularly something like appearing in a movie. It's possible that in a few years she might have the time and energy to pursue something like that, but for the more immediate future, it's going to be singing all the way. And why not? There's so much for her to explore. The label is enthusiastically calling her their Barbra Streisand, which hopefully means she'll have a fairly free hand to try all manner of music, and all different avenues of performing it. For the moment she's pursuing a relatively well trodden path, the one of the teen star, but the future holds any number of possibilities.

With *Christina Aguilera* a major hit, she's become established in people's minds. But it's worth remembering that this is just a beginning. The record has merely scratched the surface of what Christina can do. It's too early to predict where she might go next, but the options remain open. It's almost certain that she'll keep one foot in the pop camp, since that will keep her profile high, but anything and everything else is fair game.

One thing she's certainly considered is a Spanish-language album. She's fluent in the language, and has a deep love of the music. She'd certainly like the chance to explore salsa music on record, for the challenges it can offer a singer. With Latin music in general increasing in popularity, not just in America, but everywhere—in the early fall of 1999 almost half the British top twenty was Latin-influenced—something like that could be a very good move. And it wouldn't be exploitative. Christina may not have much contact with her father, but there's no denying her Latin roots. Fausto Aguilera might not have much to do with his daughter's life, but there's no denying that Christina is half-Ecuadorian. It's something she's never even tried to deny. Had that been the case, she'd have taken her mother's maiden name (Fidler), or her stepfather's last name (Kearns). But she's proud of who she is, and the possibility of fully exploring those roots would be something to be relished. There's a good chance that will happen. Even if there's not a whole album, it seems very likely that there will at least be a Spanish version of "I Turn to You" appearing fairly soon.

While Christina had a few dates lined up for the fall, opening for both TLC and 'N Sync, a tour of her own still needed to be considered. In the days of pay-per-view shows on cable, as well as specials like the Disney Channel's *In Concert* series, touring, especially for younger acts, wasn't as important as it had once been. But that didn't mean it could be discounted completely. And given Christina's love of performing, it's likely that at some point she will tour as a headlining act. In all likelihood, however, that won't be for a while yet, until she's become properly established as an artist. That doesn't mean just another hit single or two, but more likely waiting until she releases another album, giving her more material to draw on for her concerts. Not that she'd be afraid of going back and singing old Etta James tunes or even Broadway standards, but those wouldn't be the things to draw in most of her audience. A second album, and two or three more big singles, would make her into a real, certified box-office draw, the kind who could headline good-sized venues, and who could draw a strong cross section of people to her shows. Because, although Christina has been helped by the popularity of teen artists, and the openness of people toward them, that really isn't how she should be defined. Her appeal is to a very wide range. As great a pop single as "Genie in a Bottle" may be, she shouldn't be judged solely on that. Anyone who can thrive on the risk of playing Lilith Fair (and for a "pop" singer to do that was a real risk—she could easily have been booed off the stage before she'd sung a note) lives to take chances with her music, and not put all her eggs into one stylistic basket.

At the same time, there was a danger in diversifying too far, too fast—she could have easily lost her first audience, and she didn't want that. Christina might not have started out loving pop music, but it had become a part of her over the years, and it was something she truly enjoyed now. She had no wish to totally remove herself from it.

She understood that success had made her something of a role model for girls, and that was something she took very seriously. To have younger girls looking up to her, possibly trying to emulate her, was a responsibility, and it colored everything she did. While some said the lyrics of her songs seemed too sexy, she defended them quite vocally as female empowerment, with others simply having taken them the wrong way. She wanted respect for girls, as well she should! She also wanted equality. If it was okay for the boy bands to make particular dance moves or sing certain types of lyrics, why should the girls be dissed for doing exactly the same thing? Fair was fair, after all.

It was an issue she felt very strongly about, not only because it affected her personally, but because it reflected on every girl. If Christina fought for and won a few things for her gender, then it would benefit all of them, which was why she was willing to be a little outspoken if necessary. While it might not be considered feminism as such, it was, in some ways, a continuation of the "girl power" revolution the Spice Girls had started a few years before. At the time, not too many people had taken the phrase too seriously, but the girls had obviously been listening, and were acting on it. It was a real, tangible thing. Every girl had experienced problems simply because she was a girl, and it was time to take the power into their own hands, to stand up and make sure they were listened to.

It was important, not just for now, but also for the future, and the fact that Christina not only recognized it, but was also willing to do something about it showed just how mature and sensible her view of the world really was. It would be easy to simply be carried away by the sudden fame and fortune (not that she wasn't enjoying herself: once she passed her driver's test, she planned on buying a Porsche for herself), but she wasn't letting it all go to her head. Her feet remained firmly stuck on the ground.

Life had become good for her, and if she could open people's eyes and minds a little bit, then maybe it could improve for other women, too. For, while the industry might have perceived of her as a girl, she was a woman, in every way, including legally. And that was something she wasn't about to forget. She had a voice, and she was willing to raise it to try to get things done to help other women. It was noble of her, and probably no one would have thought twice if she hadn't said anything. She didn't get up on a soapbox, either, but just pursued it quietly and firmly.

It was simply one more facet of her personality, which was as complex as anyone else's, and probably just as full of contradictions. And why not? None of us really makes sense; the pieces never fit together with complete logic.

To some guys, it might have seemed illogical that Christina could talk about female equality and still enjoy the traditionally girlie things like hair, clothes, makeup, and nails. But that only proved they were living in another age altogether. None of those things made you less of a woman. Having a good do didn't mean you'd lost your brains.

And Christina had a very recognizable do. Granted, it was a bit of a variation on the one Jennifer Aniston had made popular a couple of years before, but Christina wore it with much more flair and style (and it looked better on a blonde, somehow). Being gorgeous didn't hurt her either. Yes, she liked makeup, particularly the stuff sold by MAC, but what girl doesn't use makeup? Her nails were always carefully done—her appearance was carefully considered. But then again, she was in the public eye now. She *had* to look good. And that meant clothes, too. Having such a long midriff, it was perfectly natural that Christina would want to show it, so she tended to go for crop tops, halters, and hip-hugging pants and skirts. It helped especially to make her seem taller than her natural five feet two inches, which was fairly petite.

Christina particularly liked the fashions of Dolce & Gabbana, and modeled them in a couple of editions of

Teen People. And they loved her too, as well they might. She was a very visible model for them, turning everywhere, whether she was hosting a program on MTV, or presenting an award at the MTV Video Awards, or appearing at Disney World—a place that brought back a lot of good memories for her. She was young, vibrant, and happy, and liked to dress in a way that showed it off. So long as no one believed that made her a bimbo, everything was fine. Dressing up was fun, it was expected, and Christina had the chance—and now the money—to indulge herself. So why not? It was a chance not given to many girls.

At the same time, it wasn't going to make or break her. She could also be happy at home in a sweatshirt and jeans, relaxing with her family around her, although the opportunities to do that were becoming harder and harder to find. And she missed that. She missed the security of her bothers and sisters, her mom and stepdad, and her grandmother. She was out on her own in a very big way. Her manager was there to guide her, but even though they'd been working together for six years, he still wasn't family, and never could be. His advice was good, and he was there when she needed to talk, but it wasn't quite the same. So there were frequent phone calls home, and when there were three or four spare days, she'd hurry back to Wexford, to leave the life of a celebrity behind and just enjoy being pampered in a completely different way. But, Christina had to admit, overall she was loving every minute of what was going on. This was what it was all about, and what she'd worked toward for so long.

Wonderful as the present was, it didn't stop her thinking about the future. That might have seemed ridiculous, given all the attention she was currently receiving, but it was only natural. She was going to be around for a long time, and had lots of plans she wanted to see happen. Even though her album was barely in the stores, it was never too early to begin thinking about the next one, or at least some special Spanish-language work. The current wisdom of the record business seemed to dictate a couple of years between albums, but in Christina's case, with the music bursting out of her, it seemed unlikely that she'd be able to wait that long. There was too much musical ground she wanted to cover. A two-year gap would see her having progressed almost beyond recognition.

There was another ambition too—to write some of her own material the next time around. It wasn't uncommon; ever since the Beatles, really, people had been conditioned to think in terms of writing their own material. And it was certainly laudable, wanting to contribute more to the creative side of things. It would also make the material much more personal, giving even more emotional depth to Christina's singing. How her stuff would stack up against songs by professional writers, though, remained to be seen. One thing was for sure: only the very best songs would be picked, and Christina would be the first to admit it if hers didn't match up to the rest. Songwriting was a craft, one that could take years to master, even if you had the inspiration and talent in the first place. Christina knew enough about the way songs were structured, and about music, to be able to do it, without any doubt. But to become as good as the people whose work she'd recorded would take a long time.

Sometime in the future she also wanted to learn how to produce. That made perfect sense, because it would give her the ability and the control to transfer the music she heard in her head into a finished product. As arrangements became more complex, production became more important, with the layers of instrumentation and backing vocals. These days, much of the work was done on computer—the actual mechanics of putting tracks together. But the producer directed the sound, picked the best takes—working as something of a conduit between performer and engineer, but also as the final decision-maker on the way things should sound.

These were all things that Christina could learn, and undoubtedly would in time. By now she'd spent enough time in recording studios to have a good feel for the way producers shaped tracks, to understood what they really did. The same applied to writing. Both would take some time to truly learn, but it was probably inevitable in the long term that Christina would want to take real artistic control of her career in that manner. It was the ultimate goal of every artist, and a perfectly understandable one. But Christina was smart enough to be able to balance that with outside, objective advice. That would maintain a balance of opinion and guarantee the best possible music.

There was no doubt that Christina was firmly focused on her career, as she needed to be. Down the line, she'd be able to kick back a bit more and really have a life. But that didn't mean she planned on going through the next couple of years wearing blinders.

"My schedule doesn't allow me to have a boyfriend," she says. "But if I meet someone on the road I click with, I'll make a little time."

At least she wasn't ruling out the possibilities. There had been someone back in Wexford, but that had ended, as things do. And there had been special guys in her life before—with someone who looked so good, how could there not have been guys chasing her, even before she was a star? But she had to think first and foremost about herself. She'd always had her eyes on something bigger, and now that she'd achieved it, she had to concentrate on consolidating and furthering this career of hers, which, after all, was still pretty new. Any romance was going to come in second place to that—which could be tough on the ego of any guy Christina became involved with. But that was simply the way it would have to be.

By the middle of October, *Christina Aguilera* stood at Number Six on the *Billboard* chart, with more than two million copies sold, and "Genie in a Bottle" was at Number Seven, with over a million units shipped. But while it might have seemed to some people as if they were both on the wane (although, with the single refusing to leave the top-ten, and the album still selling like hotcakes, that would have been a very pessimistic view), Christina then got a real boost. "Genie in a Bottle" would be entering the British singles charts at Number One—something that didn't happen to very many American artists. She'd even stopped the Irish girl group, B*witched, from having their fifth consecutive single enter the charts at the top position, which was a remarkable achievement. What it meant was that another country was realizing just how good Christina was, and that she really was becoming an international star. Unlike some of the boy bands who'd preceded her, and who'd made their name overseas before hitting at home, Christina had started off as a solo star in America and was now branching out, taking exactly the opposite direction (which was as much a comment on the way musical attitudes had changed in the U.S. as anything else). By the turn of the millennium, she would be known all over the world. And she really was going to become the diva of the millennium. She'd be the talent to beat as the new century began, and her star was just beginning to rise. The news about Britain was exactly what she needed to keep herself inspired—as if she needed much help anymore!

It would mean a trip across the Atlantic to appear on Britain's leading chart TV show, *Top of the Pops*, as well as talking to magazines and newspapers over there, because her success made her instant news. And after Britain would come other parts of Europe, and then Asia. Being a star in America was amazing enough. To be known globally would be totally awesome—and it was almost certain to happen.

Would her career really emulate Mariah's? It was too early to say, but that was the benchmark. It had to be. But it was possible that Christina would take more artistic chances than her heroine, who'd stayed largely in the mainstream before moving in the direction of hip-hop. However, by remaining in the public eye, and releasing good records, there was no reason why Christina couldn't follow in Mariah's footsteps. Ten years younger than her idol, she might well end up becoming the voice of her generation, as Mariah was of hers. And in turn, that would make Christina into a role model for some young singer who would come along in another decade, who was even now singing in talent shows and trying to get ahead, and maybe being ridiculed at school for it.

In many ways, Christina Aguilera represents the new America. Like millions of others, she's of Latin descent, but completely American in thought, word, and deed. She has ambitions and dreams that have lifted her from the ordinary (although she did confess to sometimes dreaming of an ordinary job—working the drive-thru at a fast food restaurant!) to make her someone for girls to look up to. So far it's been about drive and persistence, never giving up, even in the face of adversity. There have been setbacks, and times when it's seemed as if every step forward has quickly been followed by two back, but she's never allowed herself to be discouraged for long. There have been big breaks, it's true, but none of them would have happened unless she'd had talent and ambition—and the ability to dream.

Even now, it's being reflected in the music people listen to, as a real Latin influence pervades the charts. And that makes Christina, with her Latin heritage, the perfect star for today and tomorrow. Her blond looks made her the typical all-American girl, but her name revealed where she came from. She crossed boundaries, not just as a singer, but as a person. And she'd never tried to hide that heritage. It was who she was, and she was fiercely proud of it. She's absorbed not only Latin music, but a veritable history of black music, from blues to R&B to soul and gospel, which gives her a skill and understanding far beyond her years, and the ability to draw on a great deal when it comes to delivering a song.

And then, of course, there were those movie offers. If someone like Jennifer Lopez could move from being a movie star to a singing star, why couldn't Christina go the other way? With her fame continuing to grow, the offers were coming in thick and fast. Working on *The New Mickey Mouse Club* had given her acting experience. She had the looks to carry it off, there was absolutely no doubt of that, and she was certainly photogenic. For the moment, at least, it was completely out of the question, however. Music had always been her foundation, her rock, and she was going to focus on that, not be distracted by anything else.

The other question was, did she even want to be a

movie star? It was flattering to be asked, of course, but was it really her? At heart she was what she'd always been—a singer. And really, that was enough for her. Music satisfied her. It had been her comfort when she was down, it had helped her through the bad times, and now it was leading her into the best times of her life. Her dreams had always involved a career in music. She'd never even considered films. And so, lovely as it all sounded, it was unlikely that she'd be going for more screen tests anytime soon—if she even went at all.

Christina was a celebrity now, and with that came all sorts of other demands on her time. At the beginning of October, when she was at Disney World, she'd had to schedule a special session to accommodate all the photographers who wanted to shoot her picture. While it was understandable, really—she was hot, and so pictures of her were hot, too—it took away from what really mattered to her, which was the music. That was why she'd begun, and that was what would keep her going. Unfortunately, it simply went with the territory. Everyone who'd become even marginally famous had been forced to deal with exactly the same thing. Once she was out there, she became public property. She dealt with it all very graciously, giving people what they needed, not throwing tantrums or getting mad. She understood that it was a part of her job now, and that her job description had expanded from merely singing the moment "Genie in a Bottle" became a hit. She'd learned a lot in the last year, not only about the way the business really worked, but also about herself, about what she wanted and didn't want, and about what she could and could not do. She'd grown by leaps and bounds, sometimes even surprising herself; there were times she felt a great deal older than eighteen.

But it was an exciting time,.and it all thrilled her. Not just for now, but for all those possibilities of the future, when anything could happen, for all the directions in which her music could go.

One thing that truly could happen, and which had been a dream of hers for many years, was the idea of Christina singing a duet with Mariah Carey. Their voices would complement each other well, and both do have true singers' voices, controlled and with a good range. To hear them work around each other would be a thrill, especially if the material was in more of an R&B vein, which seems to particularly suit Christina's inflections.

There was another long-standing dream she hoped to realize, too. While producing herself would be wonderful, she knew that an objective pair of ears was always better at judging material and performances. But Christina would love to produce other artists someday, to try her hand on the other side of the studio. She had a much better understanding now of how the recording process worked, and what a producer contributed. While there was still a lot for her to learn, she would be willing to put in the time to absorb the knowledge—at least as soon as she had any time!

More immediately, though, her free time was taken up with learning to drive. For some reason, it was something she'd never done in Wexford, back when she was sixteen. She'd had some lessons, but not enough to go for her driver's test. Now that was something of a priority for her, her "normal thing" to do in order to help stay grounded among the publicity and the touring. Of course, it would also mean she could buy that Porsche she had her eye on. But keeping a Porsche in the traffic jam known as Manhattan wouldn't be the best idea, so in all likelihood it would live in Wexford—giving her even more incentive to visit her family.

Life was full of dreams and possibilities right now, and it said a lot that Christina was keeping them alive among the flurry of activity that made up her days and nights these days. For all intents and purposes, her life had already become a dream come true, the type of thing so many girls wish for at night. But Christina was growing and evolving at a rapid rate. It was apparent, for example, in the way she'd changed her do from the CD cover, letting it grow out to her shoulders. It would have been easier to have kept it as it was—and it would have made her a lot more recognizable. But she had to be herself. She wanted to be recognized, and that had happened; now she was moving on and being herself. To be fair, *not* being recognized so much gave her more freedom, but really it was about looking the way she wanted to look.

"It's a dream come true that people are responding in such a positive way to my music," Christina said, after her single hit the charts. "At first, I was a little afraid that some people might not completely get where I'm coming from—particularly with 'Genie in a Bottle.' " But, she pointed out, "It's time for something different. It's time that music makes kids feel confident and secure. And I'm looking forward to reaching out and touching as many of them as possible."

Obviously, she's succeeded, even if she remains the girl who sleeps with the light on, because she's afraid of the dark, or finds herself asked by hotel bellhops in strange cities whether she's on vacation (because she looks so young), when she's had the top single and album in the country.

She's achieved a great deal since *Mulan*, and truly

come out of her shell as a singer and a person. She has style and flair to match her voice—which has also grown beyond belief. But underneath it all she remains exactly the same person she's always been: warm, generous, and sometimes a little afraid.

That yet another of the Mouseketeers could become a major star says a lot for the Disney show, and the way its producers spotted and helped develop talent. Along with Justin, JC, Britney, and Keri, Christina is the fifth member of the cast to have made it big. No wonder a generation of kids is lobbying Disney to bring back the show, which would, of course, nurture a new generation's talent.

For Christina, though, all that is memories and a collection of videos now. She has the present and the future to concentrate on, and she's been doing a very fine job of it. But she knows what she wants, and she's always been determined to get it. And there's little doubt she will.

Chapter Ten

It's a long way from Staten Island to the top of the charts. And a long way from singing to a group of stuffed animals to entertaining crowds in the thousands. It's a road not many people can take, but Christina Aguilera has managed it very successfully.

To her it seems like it's taken forever to get where she is today, and the road has often wound back on itself, with plenty of diversions. But in fact she's achieved fame at a remarkably young age. While most of the people she knew were still completing their final year of high school and thinking about how they'd spend the summer before college, she had a hit single. And before those former companions of hers could even move into the dorms, she had a Number One album. It's a safe bet that Christina will never forget the summer of 1999.

But it's also a safe bet that she'll remember all the summers that follow, as her star continues to rise. She's one of the very few young singers around with the kind of voice that can really stay the course and last. A decade from now she'll still be around, covering all the musical bases, as much an icon to her generation as Mariah is to hers, and an inspiration to those who follow her. That might be a big weight to put on some small young shoulders, but it already seems quite clear. Vocalists with her power, control, and skill come along all too rarely, and once they do surface, they stay around. People recognize real quality, and that's exactly what Christina has. Star quality. Something that just can't be denied.

The will to sing, and the need to sing, have been with her all her life, as natural to her as breathing, really. From the time she was able to talk, she's done it, whether it was with a shampoo bottle, a hairbrush, or a real microphone. Many people might dream of becoming singers, but there are very few to whom it's always been a completely normal part of life. Like Christina, those few are gifted with remarkable voices, instruments they can work and develop and make into something expressive and exquisite.

It's notable, however, that Christina didn't begin to do too much with hers until she was settled in Pennsylvania. Until then her life had been a whirlwind, the typical situation of the child of an army man, moving from place to place, never quite sure where she was or where she'd be next, and never being in one place long enough to make any close friends, or put down any roots.

In Wexford she could develop some security, knowing that the family wouldn't be leaving town any time soon. She might have lost her father, but the rest of her family was there, and in due time she gained a loving and caring stepfather in Jim Kearns. With that support, as well as her brothers and sisters and grandmother, Christina was able to push forward.

In retrospect, singing at block parties might not have seemed like such a big deal, but this was tremendously important in Christina's development. It was her first taste of performing for any type of audience, and it helped give her confidence. Of course, no one was about to boo her off the stage there, and being young and cute worked in her favor, just as it would when she graduated to the very big time of singing the national anthem at major league sporting events, which wasn't too far in the future.

For someone so young, to be faced with a stadium full of people, it must have been nerve-wracking. There was always the thought that she'd forget the words, or hit the wrong note. But Christina has probably never hit a wrong note in her life. She'd rehearsed and prepared for those times, and she made sure she was completely ready, nerves shoved to one side, just singing her heart out and leading the crowds. They were major days in her life, and understandably so. But instead of a climax, they were just steps along the way.

Probably the first real turning point in her career was her appearance on *Star Search*. Although she didn't win, it did at least let her know that there was a future for her, and that she'd bested a lot of people just to make it to the program, which put her well ahead of the pack. The fact that she used the money she won to buy a small, portable PA system so she could entertain people, spoke volumes about her desires, even back then. It wasn't something most eight-year-olds would even think about, let alone seriously consider. She might not have fully understood it, but even then Christina's ambitions were firmly in place.

The fact that little happened for a few years after that had to be disheartening—although not as bad as the problems she faced from schoolmates, and her mother underwent at the hands of jealous neighbors—but it did give her a chance to listen and work at her craft. And from that point on, that's exactly what she did, and still does. Listening to the great singers, in every possible style, makes for an excellent education, and emulating them, even if it's only in your bedroom, helps stretch your voice. Christina listened hard and long, and learned very quickly, taking things from soul and blues, and quickly developing a great admiration for blues singer Etta James that would show up in her own later work and style, as would everything else she'd taken in along the way, and that she'd managed to make her own.

That was a great step in itself. Every singer has influences, but all too often young singers just copy the people they admire, rather than absorbing the ideas to create a style of their own. That Christina could sound like herself so early on showed incredible development. She got the chance to show exactly what she could do when she was finally picked to become a member of *The New Mickey Mouse Club*. It had been two years between her audition and her selection, which gave her time to go a long way—she was still traveling very quickly as a singer, learning all the time. In the two seasons she spent on the show, she got to sing several leads—a mix of pop and R&B covers, including Toni Braxton, which definitely appealed to Christina's somewhat bluesy leanings—as well as being part of the ensemble.

It was a learning experience beyond compare. For the two summers she spent in Orlando filming the series, she was incredibly happy.

"I was there for two seasons with Britney Spears and Justin and JC from 'N Sync. We all became like brothers and sisters," she says. And it was like having two extended lessons in becoming a real professional. With a whole season to film each summer, there could be no fooling around; everyone had to get to work, and work very hard. That didn't worry Christina one bit. In fact, she reveled in it, and once the summers were over, and it was back to Pittsburgh, there was a very real sense of deflation.

The second season was undoubtedly hard, knowing it would be the last, and that she'd be losing the friends she'd so recently acquired. But there was at least one compensation, in the form of Steve Kurtz, a man who'd seen her on the show and wanted to become her manager. That was one further step to becoming a real professional, even if Christina was too young to consider that move just yet. Still, simply knowing that she had a manager, that someone outside her family believed in her future, was a huge boost, at a time she really needed one. She'd come to believe that singing really could be her future, that her talent was something very special, although she wasn't stuck up about it. It was something she'd been given, that she felt obliged to make the most of.

The kids back in Wexford hadn't exactly been supportive of Christina's success. In fact, they gave her such a hard time that she transferred schools—never easy to do, even at the best of times. And the resentment would persist, even after she eventually left to be tutored while she was making her album. These days, though, given the fact that she's achieved certified stardom, she wonders what the reaction from her former classmates would be.

"If I were to go back now, I'd get a little more love," she muses. "I don't know how sincere the love would be, though."

But she did have her friends and her family. Her mother had always been behind her, every step of the way (indeed, today Shelly runs Christina's fan club, and remains involved in her oldest daughter's career), and her stepfather was also totally encouraging. Without them there, it might all have petered out to nothing. And for a while, with little happening, it seemed as if that might be the case.

But pushes can come from the strangest direction. Christina had never envisaged herself as a star in Japan, but that was her next move, after being picked to record a duet with Japanese pop star Keizo Nakanishi. To hold a record with her name on it, then to go and tour over there behind it, was exactly what she needed.

And though she didn't yet know it, Christina had another big supporter in America—Ron Fair, the head of A&R at RCA records. Her manager had sent him a demo tape she'd made, and he was impressed by her voice, but couldn't really do anything with her—yet. Still, he remained aware of her name, and the way things were going with her. In fact, he was the one who alerted the Disney people to her talent when they were looking for a young singer to record a ballad for the soundtrack of *Mulan*.

The fact that she had all these people working on her behalf definitely helped. Without those contacts she might now be another college student full of hopes and dreams. But it should never be forgotten that the bottom line is Christina's own talent. She was the one who could hit high E above middle C and did so on her very amateurish demo tape for Disney; she was the one who proved in their studios that she had what they were looking for.

Having promise was fine, but at some point you had to be able to deliver, and Christina was more than ready to deliver. And in return, she got the biggest gift of all—her own recording contract.

That's brought her to where she is today, to the top of the charts, to being in demand for everything. Maybe her album didn't show her in the light in which she'd always imagined herself, but there's no doubting its success—anyone who can sell two million copies of an album in just five weeks is *popular*.

Her success had made anything possible for Christina in the future. Her album places her not as some disposable singer of dance-pop, but as a real diva, someone with a true voice whose star will continue to rise in the coming years. That she can tackle anything is immediately apparent, whether it's pop, ballads, R&B, or whatever. That puts her in a class of one for her generation. Not only does she have the ability to last, she also has the determination. She's worked long and hard, and waited to have her opportunity, and she's taken full advantage of it.

Not only that, but she's been more than willing to take risks—like playing the Lilith Fair, performing to an audience that definitely wasn't on her side when she took the stage—they hadn't come to see some fluffy pop singer—but who were won over by the time she finished. That was a major victory, getting out there with just a piano backing her and doing music that she loved, rather than what was on her album. It was a move most brand-new stars would be afraid to make, and it speaks volumes about Christina the singer, and the lover of music.

Her tours in support of her album won't be like that—she'll be there giving the people what they want to hear—but it wouldn't be too astonishing to have her throw in one or two surprises, to toss in a curveball to keep the audience on their collective toes. It would also keep her from becoming too defined, which is the last thing she wants.

And if Christina does release the Spanish album she's been considering—if she does, it might well be all salsa, a music she loves—it won't be because Latin rhythms are hot and getting hotter (in fact, her first Spanish release will be a single, and probably a ballad). It will be her getting in touch with her roots, much in the same way Jennifer Lopez has. In other words, she'll be doing it for the right reasons, not out of sheer crass commercialism.

These are exciting times for her. Just when it seemed things couldn't get any better, there was something new and more brilliant for Christina—from a recording contract to a Number One single to a Number One album that sold in the millions. But it's something she needs to get used to—as much as anyone can ever get used to that—because it's going to continue for many years. She will be the new Mariah, the new Whitney, but there'll also be a lot of herself in the mix. Her record company likes to refer to her as the new Barbra Streisand, and with her love of show tunes, it's possible she'll also take the Broadway route at some point. But right now, anything and everything is open to her. The possibilities are endless, and in many ways, it's all up to her. She has the time and the talent to do it all. The genie is out of the bottle now, and she's not going back.

Discography

"All I Wanna Do"—Keizo Nakanishi and Christina Aguilera (Japan only) (1995–6)

Mulan Original Soundtrack (June 1998)
"Reflection"

"Genie in a Bottle" (June 1999)

Christina Aguilera (August 1999)
"Genie in a Bottle"/ "What a Girl Wants"/ "I Turn to You"/ "So Emotional"/ "Come on Over (All I Want Is You)"/ "Reflection"/ "Love for All Seasons"/ "Somebody's Somebody"/ "When You Put Your Hands on Me"/ "Blessed"/ "Love Will Find a Way"/ "Obvious"

Pokémon: The First Movie Original Soundtrack "We're a Miracle"

"Genio Atrapado" (Spanish version of "Genie in a Bottle")

Christina on the Web

There are plenty of websites dedicated to Christina Aguilera, and every time you check, there seem to be a few more. This is a sampling of the best currently around.

OFFICIAL SITES:
RCA's Christina Site (www.peeps.com/christina) offers a bio, pictures, and a wide variety of materials.

The Fan Club Site (www.Christina-A.com) is just that, a way to join the fan club.

UNOFFICIAL SITES:
Christina Aguilera Fan Flash Site (www.christina-aguilera.com) promises lots of bells and whistles, and it has them, although it takes a while to load, and you're going to need the Shockwave plug-in.

MJ's Christina Aguilera site (christina-aguilera.virtualave.net) has plenty of info, and even offers a message board.

Christina Aguilera UK (www.christina-aguilera.co.uk) is also slow loading, and also needs Shockwave, even just to see what's going on.

Absolute Christina Aguilera (<u>mtvpages.interspeed.net/ aguilera</u>) is brought to you by those people at mtv-pages. Not much original work, and nothing you can't find elsewhere.

A-Z of Christina Aguilera (<u>www.azaguilera.free-online.co.uk</u>) looks promising, but isn't as thorough as the title might make you hope.

Christina Online (<u>christina.virtualave.net</u>) is an excellent fan site, lots of information. Highly recommended.

GET THE 411 ON YOUR FAVORITE SINGERS!

B*WITCHED
0-312-97360-8___$4.99___$6.50 Can.

BACKSTREET BOYS
0-312-96853-1___$3.99___$4.99 Can.

BRANDY
0-312-97055-2___$4.99___$6.50 Can.

FIVE
0-312-97225-3___$4.99___$6.50 Can.

LAURYN HILL
0-312-97210-5___$5.99___$7.99 Can.

RICKY MARTIN
0-312-97322-5___$4.99___$6.50 Can.

THE MOFFATTS
0-312-97359-4___$4.99___$6.50 Can.

98°
0-312-97200-8___$4.99___$6.50 Can.

N SYNC
0-312-97198-2___$4.99___$6.50 Can.

BRITNEY SPEARS
0-312-97268-7___$4.99___$6.50 Can.

Get the sizzling inside story on the hot
young star of song and screen

Brandy

SITTIN' ON TOP OF THE WORLD
ANNA LOUISE GOLDEN

Named one of the "21 hottest stars under 21" by *Teen
People* magazine, Brandy, the chart-topping singer and
star of TV's *Moesha*, is one of today's hottest young
talents—a bright, headstrong woman who handles the
hurdles of stardom with major maturity, while enjoying life like an ordinary teenager (she talks for hours
on the phone, shops up a storm, and *loves* McDonald's
french fries!). Get the 411 on this award-winning
superstar and her life in front of the camera, in back of
the microphone—and *behind* the scenes.

WITH EIGHT PAGES OF FABULOUS PHOTOS!

GET ALL THE COOL FACTS ON YOUR FAVORITE CELEBS!

MATT DAMON
0-312-96857-4___$4.99___$6.50 Can.

SALMA HAYEK
0-312-96982-1___$4.99___$6.50 Can.

JENNIFER LOPEZ
0-312-97085-4___$4.99___$6.50 Can.

JENNIFER LOVE HEWITT
0-312-96991-0___$4.99___$6.50 Can.

EWAN McGREGOR
0-312-96910-4___$5.99___$7.99 Can.

WILL SMITH
0-312-96722-5___$4.99___$6.50 Can.

JAMES VAN DER BEEK
0-312-97226-1___$5.99___$7.99 Can.